Chung Do Kwan

— Chung Do Kwan —

The Power of Tae Kwon Do

C. Alexander Simpkins, Ph.D.

&

Annellen M. Simpkins, Ph.D.

Tuttle Publishing

Boston • Rutland, Vermont • Tokyo

First published in 2002 by Tuttle Publishing, an imprint of Periplus Editions (HK) Ltd., with editorial offices at 153 Milk Street, Boston, Massachusetts 02109.

Library of Congress Cataloging-in-Publication Data

Simpkins, C. Alexander.
  Chung do kwan : the power of tae kwon do / C. Alexander Simpkins and Annellen M. Simpkins.— 1st ed.
    p. cm.
  Includes bibliographical references.
  ISBN 0-8048-3297-8 (pbk.)
  1. Tae kwon do. I. Simpkins, Annellen M. II. Title.

GV1114.9 .S56 2002
796.815'3—dc21   2002020305

Distributed by:

North America, Latin America &
Europe
Tuttle Publishing
Distribution Center
Airport Industrial Park
364 Innovation Drive
North Clarendon, VT 05759-9436
Tel: (802) 773-8930
Fax: (802) 773-6993

Asia Pacific
Berkeley Books Pte Ltd
130 Joo Seng Road
#06-01/03 Olivine Building
Singapore 368357
Tel: (65) 6280-1330
Fax: (65) 6280-6290

Japan & Korea
Tuttle Publishing
Yaekari Bldg., 3F
5-4-12 Ōsaki, Shinagawa-ku
Tokyo 141 0032
Tel: (03) 5437-0171
Fax: (03) 5437-0755

First edition
05 04 03 02   9 8 7 6 5 4 3 2 1

Design by Stephanie Doyle
Printed in the United States of America

We dedicate this book to our parents, Nat and Carmen Simpkins and Herbert and Naomi Minkin, to our children, Alex and Alura, and to our teacher, Grandmaster Duk Sung Son, who continues to communicate his wisdom and the spirit of Chung Do Kwan to the world.

Contents

Acknowledgments

We would like to acknowledge Grandmaster Duk Sung Son for teaching us Chung Do Kwan and for giving us a firm foundation in the martial arts.

We would like to thank Master Dong Hoon Kim for his input and Grandmaster Hae Man Park for the interview he granted us. We also would like to thank all the Chung Do Kwan practitioners who shared their insights and furthered our understanding over the thirty-five years that we have been involved in this style. Any omissions or errors are our own.

Introduction

Chung Do Kwan is a Tae Kwon Do style known for its tremendous power. Along with this intense strength and focus comes a profound ability for self-control. Controlled force has many benefits not only for martial arts practice but also for living a strong, well-focused life. Anyone who sincerely studies this art can enhance their power and focus while remaining balanced and centered.

Chung Do Kwan also has historical interest. Because Chung Do Kwan was the first of the Tae Kwon Do *kwans* (schools) to form in Korea, traditional Chung Do Kwan practice sheds light on the early traditions of Tae Kwon Do. Many modern Korean martial arts practitioners can trace part of their roots back to Chung Do Kwan.

This book is written for anyone who is interested in the martial arts. Beginners who would like to start training in a martial art will find this style a straightforward way to begin. More experienced practitioners from any style may be interested in adding power to their technique. Tae Kwon Do students from all kwans may find it interesting to learn about one of the traditional roots of their art. We encourage you to use these methods as fits your needs.

Many innovations and changes have been made over the years but there is much to be gained by practicing these traditional methods. May you find many physical and mental benefits and satisfactions from practicing, and make your own discoveries as you travel on your personal path to power!

How to Use This Book

The chapters can be read from start to finish, or they can be read by section to learn a specific technique or skill. Instructions are placed throughout to guide you in experimenting for yourself. We have also offered supplementary exercises to help you enhance your skills.

~ PART I ~

THE SPIRIT OF CHUNG DO KWAN

— 1 —

The Tradition Begins

Confucius said, "I am not one who was born in the possession of knowledge; I am one who is fond of antiquity, and earnest in seeking it there."

Confucian Analects

Legendary Origins

Many forms of martial arts are intimately intertwined with the belief that their origins come from Buddhism. The Buddhist monk Bodhidharma (440 to 528), the founder of Zen Buddhism, is also considered the legendary founder of modern martial arts.

In India, Bodhidharma was the devoted pupil of the Buddhist teacher Pranatara. On his deathbed, Pranatara asked his student to promise he would make the long journey to China to teach meditation and the enlightenment of Buddhism. Even though the trip was dangerous, Bodhidharma kept his promise. He traveled across difficult terrain, where wild animals and ruthless robbers were a constant threat. Bodhidharma was a peaceful monk, and he carried no weapons; however, he did learn how to defend himself by carefully observing how the animals protected themselves. By imitating the movements of the animals he saw during his long journey, he was able to keep himself healthy and safe.

When Bodhidharma arrived at the Shaolin Temple in China, he found that the Buddhist monks had become weak and unhealthy from sitting in daylong meditation. This was not the point of Buddha's original teachings, and Bodhidharma tried to transmit the original enlightenment of Buddha: awake and aware meditation. But the frequently weak, passive monks were unable to grasp his teachings. In order to teach the monks, he devised a series of movements drawn from the animals to communicate meditation through dynamic action. As the monks began performing the patterns, they became healthier, more alert, and eventually found enlightenment, while engaging in positive action.

The practice of martial arts flourished in the monasteries, and as Buddhism was transmitted to Korea, so too were the associated martial arts.

Early Martial Arts in Korea

Between 37 B.C. and A.D. 668, Korea was divided into three kingdoms: Koguryo, Paek-je, and Silla. This period was violent, as the three kingdoms constantly battled with each other and their neighbors. During this time Buddhism was transmitted from China to Korea, bringing with it its message of peaceful enlightenment. Koguryo was the first Korean kingdom to accept Buddhism, in A.D. 372. Buddhism was welcomed into Silla and officially recognized in 527. Soon Buddhist monasteries were scattered throughout Korea, and monks became sources of Chinese Buddhism, Confucianism, knowledge of the *I-Ching (Book of Changes)*, and the martial arts. These warrior monks greatly influenced Korean thought and culture, helping the practice of martial arts to evolve over time.

For a long time, martial arts were connected primarily to the monasteries, but martial arts expanded into the military with Chin Hung (540 to 576 A.D.), king of the Silla kingdom. He formed an elite officer corps called Hwa Rang Do. Young men, drawn from the best of society, practiced the usual sports of archery and horsemanship and underwent careful mental and physical development through martial arts. These men also trained in cultural, religious, and ethical values; they lived by a code of honor partly drawn from Confucianism. The code consisted of:

1. Loyalty to the king,
2. Faithfulness to friends,
3. Devotion to parents,
4. Bravery and a vow to never retreat in battle,
5. A prohibition against the needless killing of any form of life.

In 688, under the leadership of Hung, the Silla kingdom conquered the Koguryo and Paek-je kingdoms and unified Korea under one government. Many people attribute the success of the Silla in part to the Hwa Rang Do.

The peaceful Silla period, which lasted until 935, allowed for creative cultural development. Martial arts known as Tae Kyun were practiced as part of the monastic life. This influence can be seen in the carving of two giant warriors who face each other in a martial arts stance, carved into a tower wall of a Buddhist temple in Kyungju, Silla's capital (Cho 1988, 15). Martial arts also continued to be practiced by the military Hwa Rang Do. Eventually the Hwa Rang Do became identified with Tae Kyun, giving Korean martial arts an even deeper philosophical root.

Tae Kyun grew in popularity, and by the time of the long-lived Koryo dynasty (935 to 1392), it was widely practiced by the military. Military training incorporated martial arts, helping to instill in the soldiers strong, brave spirits, which have become a source of inspiration for Koreans today.

The Yi dynasty, (founded 1392) brought a long period of peace and prosperity to Korea, which was still united as one kingdom. The practice of Tae Kyun expanded from the military to the general public, who engaged in it for health and sport. It was during this time that *Muye Dobo-tongji* by King Chongjo, the first known illustrated Korean book on martial arts, was published (Chun 1976, 7). Toward the end of the Yi dynasty, Tae Kyun's popularity waned as people turned to fine arts and literature. Only a small, devoted group, consisting mostly of young people, quietly carried on the traditions.

Korean Martial Arts under Japanese Occupation

Korea was involved in wars from 1894 through World War II. During the Japanese occupation of Korea, from 1910 until 1945, all martial arts, along with Korean culture and literature, were prohibited. Martial arts survived through secretive training behind closed doors. The combination of the older indigenous Korean arts with the influences from China and Okinawa that filtered in helped to reignite interest in and practice of martial arts.

The original founding fathers of Tae Kwon Do were ethical, strong, and courageous individuals who underwent tremendous challenges and hardships during the occupation years. They created a source of inner strength through the practice of a martial art that was powerful in its simple and direct techniques. Through devotion to training in a supportive atmosphere, anyone could find personal power to put to good use. Thanks to the determination of the founders of Tae Kwon Do, the Korean martial arts were reintroduced in Korea and then transmitted to the world.

The Founding of Chung Do Kwan

Chung Do Kwan, the first of the original Korean kwans, was opened by Won Kook Lee in 1944. Soon after, other kwans followed: Moo Do Kwan and Yun

Moo Kwan opened their doors. By 1945, there were five kwans, and after 1953 nine different kwans thrived.

Born in 1907, Won Kook Lee's interest in martial arts began in his teens, but because martial arts had been banned in Korea, he was not able to study seriously until he went to college in Japan. He graduated from Central University Law School, where he was able to begin his training in the martial arts. He traveled to Okinawa and China to learn more and understand the roots of martial arts more deeply. He also studied under Gichin Funakoshi, the founder of Shotokan Karate.

Lee realized that it was wrong for Koreans not to be allowed to learn the martial arts that were indigenous to their country. Upon his return to Korea, Lee tried to get permission from the Japanese government to teach martial arts, but he was turned down. He kept trying, and after the third request, he was finally granted permission and opened his first school of Tang Soo Do at the Yung Shin School Gymnasium in Seoul in 1944.

When independence came on August 15, 1945, political chaos spread across the country. Violent gangs and political groups fought in the street. Lee's students helped the police try to restore peace, but some of the rival gang members also fought with martial arts techniques. In an attempt to regain control, the government prohibited the teaching of martial arts in any public building.

In 1945, Lee moved his school to Tae Go Temple in Seoul, which is named after the fourteenth-century Korean Zen master T'aego. Lee called his art Chung Do Kwan. The usual translation is the "Blue Wave School"; another meaning is the "True Path School." Chung Do Kwan grew in popularity. Demonstrations for the public drew in more students, and by 1947 Chung Do Kwan had many members in South Korea and government support.

However, troubled times were far from over. In 1948, Korea was officially divided into two separate states: the communist North Korea and the democratic South Korea that still exist today. Amid all the instability, demoralization, and turmoil, martial arts were one of the few means of bringing together the Korean people, who needed direction and organization in the aftermath of years of occupation.

Communist armies invaded South Korea on June 25, 1950, marking the beginning of the Korean War. Many people fled south, including some Chung Do Kwan members, such as Won Kook Lee and his top students, Duk Sung Son and Woon Kyu Uhm. Lee decided to move to Japan as a political refugee, but his top students returned to Seoul.

Chung Do Kwan under Duk Sung Son

Son was appointed to be the next president of Chung Do Kwan. Under his leadership, Chung Do Kwan was rebuilt and flourished once again.

Son grew up in Seoul. His career in the fighting arts began at the age of sixteen, when he took up boxing at the local gym. He proved to be a talented fighter, rising quickly toward becoming a national champion. However, he came home each night in pain from injuries and cuts. His parents took a firm hand and would not allow him to continue to box. Rather than give up fighting altogether, he joined the Chung Do Kwan school. As Son told us (Simpkins 1993), "It was like a different world. In the boxing gym, people stole shoes and towels and the place was always dirty. But in the Chung Do Kwan school everyone was polite. There was an atmosphere of good, friendly people, all working out together. The style was no contact, so no one got hurt. I loved it!" Son attended Sensyu University, majoring in economics, but the primary focus for his life was, and continues to be, martial arts.

Son led Chung Do Kwan by encompassing powerful techniques and a dedication to strong moral principles. He also introduced many innovations that have become part of the workout. He taught the police and was the chief instructor for the Republic of Korea's Army and Military Academy.

Attempts to Unify Korean Martial Arts

It was a natural and logical step to try to raise the morale of the people through martial arts. Tae Kyun had been close to the hearts and souls of the Korean people for centuries. The ancient Hwa Rang Do had been fundamental to their code of ethics, integrity, strength of purpose, and fighting skills, and it had been instrumental in unifying Korea and repelling the takeover attempts of the past. So, the government attempted to rekindle Korea's national pride, as expressed in the people's urge to strive and achieve, in part by nationalizing the martial arts. The government also decided to train the military in Chung Do Kwan. Hong Hi Choi, a general in the Korean army, was put in charge of training the military in martial arts. He formed the Oh Do Kwan as the military kwan and later founded ITF, the International Taekwondo Federation.

The government began its effort to unify the kwans, to help unite and inspire its people. The first conference of the National Board of Advisors for Chung Do Kwan met together over dinner on December 19, 1955. Grandmaster Son was present and played a primary role in this early formulation of Tae Kwon Do, along with government officials, the media, and several other prominent martial arts leaders such as General Choi. The members of the conference decided to give their martial art a Korean name. Son said they accepted the name Tae Kwon Do because it closely resembled the name for the ancient Korean arts, Tae Kyun, and it expressed the use of the hand and the foot—Tae Kwon Do translates as "The Way of Kicking and Punching." President Syngman Rhee liked the idea, and the name was made official. It was announced in the national newspaper that all schools were to change their names to Tae Kwon Do. But some of the kwans did not want to change their names and unify, and so the name Tae Kwon Do was not universally adopted at first.

Political and social unrest continued to shake Korea. In 1961, the government was overthrown by a short-lived military coup led by General Chang. A second upheaval put in place a new military rule under General Park, who took control later that year. Democratic rule was reestablished under Park in 1963.

Some of the early masters left Korea to start organizations of their own in the United States. Son went to New York City in 1963, where he began teaching. He brought along with him other Chung Do Kwan masters, who immigrated to various parts of the United States, forming a large organization known as The World Tae Kwon Do Association. At a time when martial arts were relatively unknown to Western people, Son openly taught sincere students who wanted to learn. He was awarded the Medal of Honor by President Park of South Korea in 1965.

Woon Kyu Uhm became the next president of Chung Do Kwan in Korea. He continued in this position, training many great practitioners over the years. He was instrumental in forming the Korean World Tae Kwon Do Federation (WTF) in 1972. He is now vice president of the Kukkiwan, the governing organization of Tae Kwon Do.

Hae Man Park is an ambassador for Chung Do Kwan around the world. He is also the chairman of the Steering Committee of Korean Chung Do Kwan in Korea and was a chief Chung Do Kwan instructor for many years. The organization of Tae Kwon Do has changed in Korea. Today, all the Korean kwans are part of the broader organization of the World Tae Kwon Do Federation. The individual kwans still exist, but they are part of one system.

Now, all kwans within the Korean organization use the same forms and techniques so that the differences that distinguished one kwan from another have lessened. However, modern Korean Tae Kwon Do has retained many of the best methods of teaching from early Chung Do Kwan: basics, forms, three-step sparring, and free sparring are still practiced. As Park told us, "The old philosophy is still being applied: good mind, strong form, and get students ready for free sparring."

Chung Do Kwan Takes Root in the West

Son's World Tae Kwon Do Association grew into a large organization, spreading from coast to coast. During the 1960s, '70s, '80s, and '90s, Son personally led classes at many colleges, including West Point, Yale, Princeton, Brown, Columbia, New York University, Fordham, Stony Brook, and Providence. He also taught employees of major corporations, including IBM and Chase Manhattan Bank. Eventually there were hundreds of schools in his organization. Many of them continue to flourish.

As mentioned, all the World Tae Kwon Do Association schools share a common curriculum of basics, forms, three-step, and sparring. Son personally conducts all black belt testing so that he can oversee the quality of his students around the country. Now in his eighties, Grandmaster Son also continues to teach at his headquarters in New York City and in some of his extended locations.

Chung Do Kwon Branches Out

Many who trained at the original Chung Do Kwan school under Lee, Sung, and Uhm have settled throughout the world, keeping the art vibrant. Chung Do Kwan is practiced in the United States, Europe, South America, South Africa, and many other countries around the world. Here are some examples drawn from the many Chung Do Kwan schools and organizations that are practicing today.

Han Cha Kyo, who counts Son and Uhm as two of his primary teachers, formed the Universal Taekwon-do Federation in the Chicago area. He teaches a version of Chung Do Kwan with strong emphasis on traditional values. The Tae Kwon Do Chung Do Kwan Schools, headquartered in Tucson, Arizona, teach Chung Do Kwan in affiliation with WTF. Dong Hoon Kim, who leads these schools, originally trained in Korea under Son. Chung Do Kwan UK has schools throughout England, teaching the WTF Chung Do Kwan curriculum. They stem from the Uhm lineage.

Some Western students created their own organizations. For example, Edward B. Sell is an American grandmaster who learned Chung Do Kwan in

Korea under Uhm in the 1960s. He and his wife, Brenda, also a high-ranking Chung Do Kwan practitioner, have formed a large Chung Do Kwan organization, the U.S. Chung Do Kwan Association (USCDKA). A more recent organization, the Chung Do Kwan Alliance, was formed in 1996 and brings together various schools to practice traditional Chung Do Kwan, along with other arts. A few member schools include the Mountain View Tae Kwon Do School and Northern Arizona Martial Arts.

Some who trained under Son and Uhm became eminent martial artists who branched out and created new forms as Tae Kwon Do evolved in America. H. U. Lee, the founder of the American Tae Kwon Do Association (ATA), considers Son and Uhm to be his grandmasters (Kim 1999, 68). Jhoon Rhee, also a former student at the Korean Chung Do Kwan school, is a well-known proponent of Tae Kwon Do and physical fitness on Capitol Hill and to the world. Mohammed Ali credits Rhee with helping to improve his punch and helping him create the "accupunch" for his winning bout with Antonio Inoki in 1976 (Simpkins & Simpkins 1994, 40).

We have all greatly benefited from the founding fathers of Chung Do Kwan. The many schools and variations of Chung Do Kwan around the world have their basis in the history, philosophy, and teachings of the founders of this martial art. On the fertile ground of Western soil, Chung Do Kwan continues to grow and develop. Though each organization may have its own unique nature and agenda, they have much in common, sharing in the powerful spirit that is Chung Do Kwan Tae Kwon Do.

– 2 –

Philosophical Roots

Although Tae Kwon Do does not have a philosophy per se, its philosophy, if it had one, is most
closely akin to that of Zen if, in fact, it is not the
same thing.

Son & Clark

Chung Do Kwan has certain guiding criteria: directness, simplicity, and sincerity. These principles draw depth of meaning from their philosophical bases in
Zen Buddhism and Confucianism. As history shows, philosophy was interwoven
into the practice of Chung Do Kwan from its earliest beginnings. Practical expression of these philosophies is shown in the techniques. In this way, the performance
of the traditional martial arts such as Chung Do Kwan is more than a collection
of physical motions: Mind is involved. As you practice the art, you will begin to
understand the deeper meaning of these philosophies from direct experience.

The correct mental orientation to martial arts can enhance everything you
do. Mind in martial arts takes you from the superficial to the profound, inte-
grating your martial art into your whole personality. This gives meaning to the
idea of unity among mind, body, and spirit, so your martial art becomes a full
expression of your best capabilities in action.

Zen in Chung Do Kwan

Zen has long been known to be associated with the martial arts. (See chapter 1)
When Bodhidharma traveled to China, he had something new to teach: a pure
version of Buddhism. He stripped away all of the elaborate rituals and techniques
that had built up since Buddha's original clear teachings nearly 1000 years earlier. Bodhidharma returned to a simple approach to enlightenment: meditation.
As Bodhidharma said, "I don't talk about precepts, devotion or ascetic practices.
Once you recognize your moving, miraculously aware nature, yours is the mind
of all buddhas" (Pine 1989, 42–43).

Bodhidharma tried to communicate his radically new approach to the people of China. But few understood, because they were accustomed to the rituals and complicated practices that had become part of Buddhism. They resisted returning to a simpler way. Bodhidharma became disillusioned with teaching, and so he retired to a cave located near the Shaolin Temple in Hunan Province and sat facing a wall, meditating for nine years. Word spread of this intensely devoted monk who had great wisdom. Finally, a worthy student convinced Bodhidharma to bring his meditation methods to others. It was then that Bodhidharma began to teach the monks at the Shaolin Temple, using the martial arts movements along with meditation to bring the monks back into touch with themselves. With intense focus on every move, monks were able to enhance their alert awareness and discover the true meaning of Zen: Direct pointing at the mind of man. "Seeing into one's nature and the attainment of Buddhahood" (Simpkins & Simpkins, 1999, 45).

Chung Do Kwan embodies Zen in action. Like Bodhidharma, who meditated in the cave with absolute devotion for nine years, the spirit of Chung Do Kwan is intense and committed. Workouts have little talk and much action. Focus on every technique is most important. Modern Chung Do Kwan teachers carry on this tradition.

Simplicity and Emptiness

Chung Do Kwan was inspired by the Zen idea of simplicity—strip away everything that is unessential and return to the fundamentals. This Zen saying epitomizes Zen simplicity: "Returning to the root, we get the essence" (Blyth 1964, 101). A martial artist needs a certain basic collection of blocks, kicks, and punches. Perfect these essential techniques, and you are ready for anything. When people have too many techniques, they don't become good at any of them. Take the time to develop each move to its fullest. Techniques should be practiced so much over time that they become an integral part of being. You are your techniques and your techniques are you.

But what lies at the root of technique is an idea somewhat new to Westerners but well known in the East: emptiness. People are accustomed to thinking of something: We strive toward a goal, try to accomplish something and attain something of importance. But to Buddhists, everything is transitory. All of our striving toward material goals is ultimately fruitless and the root of all suffering. What seems so certain today will be gone tomorrow. The true nature of reality is empty.

Emptiness is not negative, nor is it a vacuum or void. Emptiness is a reservoir of potential. The usefulness of a cup is in its emptiness. Once the cup is filled, we can no longer use it. Zen practitioners learn to empty themselves of all disturbances so that they can be fully present—fully focused on the present moment. Zen master Takuin advised many swordsmen on the art of "no-mind" to improve their martial arts practice. He taught that when you have nothing in your mind you are like a wheel turning freely. When you keep your mind empty, nothing stands in the way of your reactions. Whatever you have trained yourself to do will be performed automatically, without hesitation, like a bolt of lightning.

Chung Do Kwan encourages this immediate presence, empty of all distractions. Students practice techniques very deliberately in learning the basics, forms, and three-step. But when they perform the sparring part of the workout, called free sparring, they react spontaneously. When you try to think about what your opponent might do, your mind is filled with this thought. Movements slow down because reactions are mediated by thinking. Clear your mind of all thought—be empty and fully present in the moment, and you will perform at your best. (See chapter 11, "Free Sparring.")

Meditation

The word *zen* translates as "meditation," and meditation is the cornerstone of Zen and of martial arts. Even though the members of some martial arts schools may not formally sit down to meditate, the meditative mind is an essential part of technique. The ability to perform every kick, punch, and block with nothing in mind—fully focused in the moment—is as much a mental skill as it is a physical one.

The following story illustrates the importance of meditation: A group of young martial artists visited a famous Zen master. The master asked them to demonstrate their martial arts. Proudly, they demonstrated their forms with great speed, agility, and strength. The Zen master smiled and said, "Your martial arts skills are very good, but I could beat you with my fan!" The students thought he was a foolish old man and answered with confidence, "We accept your challenge." The elder of the students bowed to the Zen master and put up his guard.

"Attack me with your strongest offense," the master urged.

The student attacked hard, but the Zen master's fan was in place as a block. The student attacked again, but the fan came up immediately in defense. Wherever the student tried to punch or kick, the Zen master's fan was always there. Finally the master touched the student in the kidney, indicating a potentially damaging blow.

The students were all mystified. "How is it that you, a monk, trained in meditation and not sword technique could be so skilled?"

The Zen master answered, "The principle is the same. I had nothing in mind to get in the way."

Even though meditation is not a part of traditional Chung Do Kwan practice, meditating on your own may help you to sharpen your mental skills for enhanced martial arts performance. Here are some different ways to learn how to let go of distractions.

NO-THOUGHT MEDITATION

Sit on the floor with your legs crossed, back straight but not rigid, eyes closed. Let your hands rest comfortably on your knees. Allow your breathing to relax. Don't think about anything. When a thought occurs to you, try to let it go and return to no-thought. Do not force it, simply allow your thoughts to settle and keep returning to not thinking. In time, you will have fewer and fewer distracting thoughts and longer periods without them. You will be able to use this clarity of consciousness to perform your martial art fully.

CLEAR-MIND MEDITATION

Imagine that your mind is like a lake. At first it is slightly cloudy, with particles floating around like thoughts filling your mind. But gradually, everything settles to the bottom, leaving the water absolutely clear and calm. Your thoughts are quiet as you imagine the clear water. Practice this until you relax your mind and allow it to clear. Use this meditation to develop your ability to clear your mind of distractions so that you can be fully present in the moment.

BREATHING MEDITATIONS

Attention to breathing can be a link between mind and body. Many forms of meditation use breathing as a pathway to deeper consciousness.

For the purposes of martial arts, learning to control breathing is helpful for making techniques more focused and ensuring that a technique is well supported by the whole body. Control of breathing can also help keep your emotions steady, even in the face of a threat. Beginning students often breathe incorrectly and run out of breath. Breath control will lead to greater endurance.

This meditation will show you how to become aware of breathing. Sit comfortably, cross-legged on the floor, with your back relatively straight but not rigid. Close your eyes. Pay attention to your breath as it moves down into your lungs, and then out again. Do not alter your breathing as you notice it, simply follow it with awareness. Do this for several minutes. When you feel finished, open your eyes. With practice, meditation becomes easier and feels more natural. Be patient.

The Confucian Philosophy of Chung—the Center

Confucianism has also had a strong influence on the development of Tae Kwon Do and Chung Do Kwan. One of the primary principles in Confucianism is called *Chung*, the Mean. The mean is the center, the balance point, like a sixth sense within our human perception. Whatever we do should be guided from the point of reference of our own center. When we align ourselves with the center, like a compass always pointing to the north, we know where to go and what to do. Correct action flows naturally when we stay close to the mean. Confucianism teaches: "The perfection of the way is already within, ready and waiting to be actualized" (Simpkins & Simpkins 2000, 69).

Chung means balance between extremes in Chinese. Confucius advised people not to get too extreme, because extremes take us further and further away from the mean—the center. The further away from the center we get, the more difficult it is to regain the mean.

In the practice of Chung Do Kwan, all techniques come from and go through the center, with balance. Punches are performed to the center, blocks sweep in to the center or out from the center. Kicks are also placed in the center.

Confucius did not tell people what the center should be for all people but advised that each person must seek the true center for him- or herself, Chung Do Kwan techniques are guided from the center, wherever that is for each individual. Where the center is depends upon your physique. In order to be centered, a tall, heavyset person will have to adopt a height and length for his stance different from that of a small, thin individual.

There are many different techniques to be learned, each with varied possibilities for application. For example, a back stance has a different balance point than a front stance. An upper target punch is centered differently from a lower target punch. Yet all techniques share in a common central principle: the center. Discover it and stay close to it. For example, beginners often make the mistake, when they punch, of extending their arm away from their centerline. As a result, the potential power that can be generated from the whole body is lost. The punch simply comes from the arm and shoulder, resulting in a much weaker technique. Your personal best must include all that you are, your whole body, working in balanced unity, for maximum power.

Confucian Values

> He who respects others is respected by others.
>
> *Mencius*

The Hwa Rang Do took on the important Confucian values such as loyalty and respect. The purposeful way of the warrior was founded on integrity. Inner strength was expressed as outer strength, manifested in action. This spirit has been passed along in the practice of Chung Do Kwan. Participants treat fellow students and teachers with respect. Like the Confucian idea of filial piety, honoring the teacher is similar to honoring one's parents. Teachers also have a responsibility to the student, to teach with wholehearted sincerity. This special relationship becomes a trust between them. Both can be raised up through the interaction, to become wiser and better, expressing virtue in action.

Sincerity and Wholeheartedness

Confucianism and Zen share the value of sincerity. Everything we do in life should be done fully, with our wholehearted commitment. The way to be sincere in thought and action is through doing things wholeheartedly, in a unified way. When people do things half-heartedly, they often do not succeed. The samurai of feudal Japan honored sincerity as one of the highest virtues. Experienced martial artists know that when they do their workouts halfway, they do not progress.

If you sincerely try with every kick, every punch, every block, distractions will disappear of their own accord. All that you should think about is what you are doing. Make each move the best you can do at the time. With nothing else in mind, you will put yourself fully into your martial art. This wholehearted attitude can affect your entire life.

Figure 2-1 *Bowing is a tradition that expresses mutual respect.*

Chung Do Kwan is a very practical and physical art. Yet, paradoxically, the physical practice of Chung Do Kwan is very spiritual. Practitioners experience this spiritual quality, but they rarely talk about it. Mind, body, and spirit form a triangle, working together. And therefore, by perfecting movements with concentration, the third element, spirit, is engaged. Hard work and sincere effort is necessary for great accomplishments in life. Strength of character, moral determination, and many positive qualities follow. Although its roots may be in Eastern philosophy, spirituality is universal. Rituals, beliefs, and practices may vary, but its essence is universal. Today, we see modern Chung Do Kwan masters and students in the West from a variety of faiths, all drawing inner strength from the regular practice of their art.

~ PART II ~

THE PRINCIPLES OF
POWERFUL TECHNIQUES

− 3 −

Where Does the Power Come From?

When the elements unite
Their focus leads to force
In blocking or striking
Their oneness is the source

C. Alexander Simpkins

Where does martial arts power come from? Martial arts power has been depicted as developing in two main ways: from soft force and from hard force. Soft styles of martial arts believe that true power comes from an inner, vital energy known as *chi*. Relaxed muscles allow the inner power from chi to flow through the body and be expressed outward as force. Hard styles are sometimes believed to rely on muscular strength alone; this strength not only wanes with age but may also become rigid, interfering with the flow of chi.

Chung Do Kwan uses hard force, but it does not fit this stereotype. Practitioners develop tremendous power that draws on both mind and body, working as one. Correct use of a number of different qualities makes techniques forceful without developing rigid muscles. Power comes from combining these many qualities in synchrony.

Grandmaster Son specified six qualities that combine to make powerful, effective techniques: focus, relaxation, accuracy, balance, speed, and strength (Son & Clark, 1992). Note that strength is only one of the qualities and not the central one. Flexibility and inner calm are just as important. By correct application of all these qualities, a smaller person can overcome a larger one. When these qualities are coordinated, you will find yourself expressing the maximum power possible for you. We will look at each of these qualities in turn.

Focus

Absolute unity of mind with action can be developed by the practice of Chung Do Kwan. Total presence in mind and body is expressed as a quality: focus. Focus is the split second when everything comes together in movement.

Figure 3-1 *The practitioner exhibits intense focus directed into his downward strike.*

Body focus uses the whole body, working correctly together. For example, at the moment when a focused punch hits the target, the body is committed 100 percent. Appropriate muscles are tight, such as the fist, wrist, arm, chest, and back. The stance must be balanced and sturdy to support the force generated by the upper body. At the instant of contact, everything is directed to the target.

But there is more to focus than the physical aspect. Similar to the internal arts practitioners, a large part of focus involves the mind. Mental concentration is foremost. Mind first, as the Zen Buddhists say, applies to every move in Chung Do Kwan.

This kind of total mental focus is seen sometimes in the midst of a crisis when people do what is normally impossible. A desperate mother is able to lift a car off a child, or a badly injured man is able to carry a stranded victim out of a burning building. In both these examples mental focus is absolute. These heroes are not thinking of the bills they have to pay, the work remaining to be done, or a relationship they are involved in. All mental effort is spontaneously directed. When questioned later, people usually report not thinking of anything—just acting. The empty, clear mind of Zen can be developed through practicing your martial art wholeheartedly. This capacity can also be enhanced by the practice of meditation. (See chapter 2 for meditation instructions.)

Breathing plays a crucial part in the mind/body unity and is a key aspect of focus. Many forms of meditation begin with focus on breathing. (See chapter 2 for breathing meditation methods). The breath is expelled sharply at the moment of focus. The force of the exhalation comes from the lower abdomen, helping to unify the upper and lower body with the mind. Correct breathing draws upon the lower abdominal region, (*tan t'ien*) a power center in many Eastern martial arts.

Relaxation

Relaxation is the counterpoint to focus in a rhythm of opening and closing, tensing and loosening. Although practitioners of Chung Do Kwan do tighten their muscles at the moment of impact, they are relaxed the moment before and the moment after the point of focus. Movements begin as a relaxed flow that culminates at the moment of focus, when muscles are tensed appropriately. After the limbs used in the technique are withdrawn, the practitioner returns to relaxation. Without a relaxed element to movements, practitioners would become rigid, unresponsive, and slow.

Learning how to relax is a skill in itself. We often feel as if the best way to relax is to distract ourselves, for example, by going out to a movie or getting lost in a good book. But another way to relax can be far more complete and satisfying: becoming more aware. Careful use of attention can help you to understand exactly where your tension is. In the same way, awareness of your muscles will help you gain control over your technique, allowing you to tense and relax at will.

In a class situation, feedback from the instructor lets you know when and how you are using your muscles—if you are not relaxing your muscles enough or if you're tensing your muscles at the wrong times. If you want to have this awareness on your own, you can try the exercise that follows. By gaining control over your entire body, you can learn how to tense and relax selected muscle groups at will. As you master the many subtleties that help you to direct and use your power efficiently and effectively, your movements will become more controlled.

RELAXATION EXERCISE

Lie on the floor and relax. Let your muscles relax as much as possible. Now tighten your arms, make fists, and hold them tight for approximately thirty seconds. Notice how your arms feel. Now completely relax all your muscles. Compare the sensations in your arms now that they are relaxed. Relax for another minute. Then tighten your arms again, keep them tight, and relax.

Try tightening your legs, holding them, and then relaxing. Keep your attention on the area you are working on. Next tighten your chest and stomach muscles, but keep the back of your body loose. Tense the muscles and then relax. Now, tense your back while remaining relaxed in your chest, arms, and legs, and then relax all over. Finally, tighten your whole body, and then relax. As you work with this exercise, by singling out specific muscle groups to tense and relax, you gain control over auxiliary muscle areas such as the back, chest, stomach—areas that are used to power your techniques. In part, cultivating awareness of sensations makes distinguishing between tension and relaxation easier. But deliberately tensing and relaxing also changes the involuntary reflex so that it becomes voluntary. Another pleasant effect of this exercise is that you can experience deep overall relaxation at will.

Accuracy

Accuracy training goes hand in hand with power training at every level. A powerful attack or block is ineffective if it is inaccurately placed. This fact is most evident when breaking wood. Even if you have a powerful strike, you will not break the board if you miss its center.

Accuracy is both a skill and a state of mind. In Chung Do Kwan, one exactly placed kick or punch could finish the encounter. Thus students should start thinking about accuracy early on. Begin with your intention. Every time you kick, punch, or block, aim at the center of an imaginary target. Vary the height of the target, sometimes high, sometimes low. Try striking from different distances, to incorporate stepping and shifting. Intend to be accurate in everything you do in basics, forms, sparring, and the three-step, and you will find yourself taking the appropriate steps to do so.

Body Awareness Exercise

Body awareness helps you place your strikes and blocks exactly where you want them. You can enhance your body awareness simply by turning your attention to your body. We often ignore this level of functioning, but it can be very helpful to the martial artist, who is always using his or her body as an expression of the art.

Lie down on the floor on your back with your arms and legs resting on the floor. Close your eyes. Focus your attention on your bodily sensations. Imaginatively trace how far it is from your fingertips to your shoulders. Sense the distance between your shoulders. Trace the distance from your hand to your shoulder. Notice how long your arms are. Then, notice how long your legs extend. How far is it from your foot to your hip? Try to let the experience become vivid. Your body image is helpful in developing an intuitive sense of distance. Learn your own perimeters. Try noticing your boundary zones during slow movements of your arms, circling outward and inward. An intuitive sense of these dimensions will help you improve your ability to control distance. Knowing how far your arms and legs reach will enable you to place your punches and kicks just where you want them to be.

No-Contact

Accuracy refers to control, and control is improved by the use of no-contact. Sparring is performed with no-touch attacks. At the black belt level, punches and kicks barely brush the clothing. The idea behind no-contact is to be able to perform a full-force blow that could do harm, but because it is carefully aimed a little distance from the target, no one gets hurt. (See chapter 11 on sparring.) The ability to maintain accurate control develops because people are not hitting or being hit. The workout itself trains this skill, as will be shown. The following exercise will get you started and can be practiced to enhance your control.

PRACTICE IN ACCURATE PLACEMENT

Stand in front of a pad in a horse stance. (See chapter 4 for stance instruction.) Extend your punch out so that it is an inch or two away from your target. Perform a series of punches without moving your feet. Try to keep a constant distance from the target. As you become more experienced, you can move closer and closer, until your full-force technique barely touches the target.

TARGETS

Whenever you punch or kick, you should consider where your attack is going. Space is divided into three basic regions: upper, middle, and lower. Upper is the area from your shoulders to your head. Middle begins at your shoulders and moves down to your belt. Lower is anywhere below the waist. These general zones are targets for offense and defense.

Defensive targets should be proportional in size to your own body. When sparring with a partner, you'll have to adjust the height of your sparring and three-step technique to the height of your partner. However, when you perform a strike or block while practicing by yourself, as in rehearsing the basics and forms, you should pick a target area measured in relation to your own body.

Aim at a target that lines up with the center of your body. This will help you to keep your shoulders square without twisting. Try to place your punch or kick exactly at this point every time, and your accuracy will improve. Aiming deliberately in practice will result in your control being automatically available when you need it.

Figure 3-2 *This punch is aimed at the upper target.*   **Figure 3-3** *This punch is aimed at the middle target.*

ACCURACY EXERCISE

Accuracy develops in response to practice. You can improve the accuracy of your aim by target practice. Hang a string from a hook in the ceiling. Tie a piece of paper, approximately three inches square, to the string, and mark an X in the center. Practice punching, kicking, and blocking, aiming at the target, stopping about one inch away. Gradually approach closer and closer, until you can barely touch the paper with your full-force technique.

Balance

Balance begins with a good stance. Chapter 4, "Stances," describes the different stances and the balance point for each. Stance is not separate from technique. Your whole body works together to perform a balanced move. Whenever you extend your force forward, you need to counterbalance it with a backward force. Otherwise, the power of your technique will throw you off balance, thereby dissipating your power. Power is balanced by the coordinated use of pushing and pulling. Each technique has its own dynamic balance to allow you to express maximum force without losing power along the way. Practice each move with attention to where your balance is and how your force might change your balance point.

BALANCE OF FORCES FROM THE CENTER

The midsection is considered the source of power and balance. By keeping your center of gravity in your lower abdomen, you will always be balanced and ready. For example, when you are in a front stance, even though your weight is more forward than backward, your lower abdomen is centered for that stance.

The lower abdominal area has a long tradition of importance in martial arts. Called the *tan t'ien* in Chinese, this area is considered an important energy center in the body. Chinese medicine uses this area to promote healing. Taoists believe that by focusing on the area located several inches below the navel, you can raise your energy and then direct it wherever you choose.

Martial artists can utilize this power in their techniques. You can draw upon the power of this area in several ways; the push-pull and hip rotation are two such exercises.

CHAMBERING AND THE PUSH-PULL THEORY

The chamber is the place where your fist rests at your side, elbow bent and pointing directly behind you. In Chung Do Kwan, the chamber is just below waist level on the hip bone. This allows the arm used in techniques to travel from chamber to full extension, a distance that is adequate to maximize your force.

Chambering offers a place for the less active hand. Whenever a force is expressed outward, the other hand moves back, with an equal and opposite force, to the chamber. Both hands work in a coordinated push-pull motion to add power to techniques.

Figure 3-4 *Chamber position is at the hip.*

This push-pull dynamic utilizes physics to advantage, allowing you to retain balance and control inwardly, while delivering power outward. Without the push-pull motion, executing a powerful technique can throw you off balance; force is dissipated away from the technique and into trying to regain the center. Beginners often make this mistake.

Hip Rotation

Some of the reaction force is generated by pulling the opposite hand back, but not all techniques allow the use of the chamber for the opposite hand. The balancing of forces can also be accomplished within your body, using hip rotation.

Correct rotation of the hips is used in blocks, hand attacks, and kicks. The movement is so subtle that an observer might not quite notice it. However, this rotation of the trunk area is an important source of power.

The hips promote an equal and opposite force by first rotating in the same direction beyond the center of the technique and then snapping back to center. This use of counter hip rotation is one of the unique features of the style.

As you begin to step into a right punch, for example, pivot your hips slightly around to the right. Your belt knot should be visible to the right of center, as shown in Figure 3-5. When the punch is past midway and you are beginning to focus, bring your hips around toward the left, with your belt knot slightly past center (Figure 3-6). At the full extension of the punch, your hips should return to center with a snap, so that your belt knot faces directly to the front. The final pivot helps stop the technique and balances the force of your punch (Figure 3-7). Let your hips rotate on a horizontal plane, without swaying up or down. Your abdominal and thigh muscles help to control the movement. Tense them as you pivot back to center to focus with a strong, balanced stance. Do not exaggerate, however. This happens naturally with correct delivery.

Speed

Newton's law of force tells us that force equals mass times acceleration. This means that the faster a mass moves, the more force it can generate. So practitioners should develop speed to increase their force. Correct application of tension and relaxation is key in speed work. If you are tight the whole way in a punch, for example, it will come out slowly. On the other hand, if you are slack and loose at the moment of impact, the punch will be weak, even if it is fast. Learn to relax during delivery and tighten at the moment of impact for maximum speed. Lighter practitioners can generate more force from speedier motion, while slower or heavier practitioners can generate force by engaging more of their mass with well-coordinated motion. Both can be effective.

Figure 3-5   Figure 3-6   Figure 3-7

RHYTHM PRACTICE

You can use music with a fairly fast beat to improve your speed. Let some music play while you are working out; you may need to experiment to find the right rhythm. Shadow box to the music, throwing punches, blocks, and kicks to the beat. Relax and allow yourself to move with the music. Then, try to have the extension of your technique correspond to the end of the beat. You may find that the music helps to inspire your motions and push you to be quicker or to incorporate different patterns or rhythms. As you get faster, you may want to use music with a faster beat. Some might prefer drums, congas, or even a metronome.

REACTION TIME

Another component of speed is reaction time. Reaction time does improve with practice. You can enhance it with this exercise. You may need to create some space in front of your television. Turn on the TV with the sound off. Stand back, in a stance where you can see the television but have room to kick or punch. Whenever the camera angle changes, throw a punch, kick, or block. Try to respond as quickly as you can. You will react more quickly with time. You may think of other variations of this exercise.

Your reaction time refers to the time it takes to respond to an attack. Reaction time will improve as your awareness is sharpened. Clearing your mind of distractions and opening yourself to the moment will help you to react quickly. Meditation can be helpful in bringing about the state of "no-mind." See the meditation instructions in chapter 2.

Strength

Practitioners naturally develop strength over time through the practice of Chung Do Kwan. Intense drilling in basics, forms, and the three-step are used to develop force and strength. But training equipment can supplement in strength building; striking a *kwon go* (a padded board known as a *makiwara* in Japanese styles) and heavy bag can be used to compliment other techniques. Instructions for the use of training equipment will be given in chapter 12. Although you can do light weight-lifting exercises and jogging to enhance your fitness level, if you spend too much time lifting weights and jogging, you may not have enough time to devote to your martial art. The Chung Do Kwan workout itself will improve cardiovascular fitness and muscular strength. Some muscular strength can be helpful, but raw physical strength is not what makes techniques effective. Only through the coordination of all the qualities we have discussed will you be able to harness your strength and make it effective. "Properly applied strength is the thing, not just brute strength" (Son & Clark 1992, 13).

ATTITUDE AND TRAINING FOR POWER

Most important for developing your power is making a sincere effort at every workout to always do your best. You will be surprised what diligent, regular practice can do, quite naturally. Sincere practice of your martial art gives back far more than you put into it. Students undergo a rebirth of the body as they come to embody the qualities they train with: strength, focus, balance, accuracy, and quickness, while also remaining relaxed and flexible. These benefits are far reaching, extending into every aspect of everyday life. Simply work out. Then power will grow naturally within you.

– 4 –

Stances

The ground means the location, the place of pitched battle. Gain the advantage and you are victorious. Lose the advantage and you are vanquished.

Sun Tzu

Chung Do Kwan requires strong stances for delivering the powerful techniques that are the hallmark of the style. Whenever you stand still, your feet should be in position, with your weight balanced between them in a certain way. For the purpose of delivering a strong punch, kick, or block, a consistent pattern is necessary so that the ground can be used as a base. Stances provide that pattern, creating a reliable foundation for techniques.

Some modern Chung Do Kwan styles have added stance variations, but all rely on a repertoire of strong, basic stances as their foundation. Practitioners repeat these stances over and over. Eventually the stances become instinctive and can be called upon for use without thought.

Each stance has stronger and poorer aspects, depending on what it is intended for or what it follows. Incorporate the most solid position for each body profile: front stance for facing front, horse stance for facing sideways, and back stance for in between. The light, mobile cat stance and X-stance serve for transitions. This covers the possibilities in a basic but complete manner.

Staying Centered

A stance exists whether you are in motion or not, whether you are shifting or still. Weight distribution is part of what defines a stance as a back stance, front stance, or horse stance, but wherever the weight lies, the center of gravity is constant. If it is kept within reasonable boundaries, you will be in balance and strong at all times.

Keep the center of gravity within the stance, not outside, and without leaning. This gives stability. A good stance is well balanced and strong, with correct foot positioning. Observe the photographs of each stance. Place your feet correctly so that you are able to position your weight between your feet.

Ready Position

In the ready position, known as *Choon-bee* (get ready), your feet should be parallel and shoulders' width apart, with your toes pointed straight ahead. Position your weight evenly between your feet, keep your body upright, and make sure your posture is straight and your head is up. Form fists, with your hands facing each other at the level of your belt knot. Your arms will be bent slightly at the elbow and facing out (Figure 4-1). Basics, forms, and three-steps begin and end in the ready position.

Being able to return to a perfect ready stance, with feet facing forward and your weight evenly balanced, teaches precision. It helps you return to your center, not just physically but also mentally: gathered and in control. In Buddhist philosophy, to return as you began brings about harmony and balance. Your mind clears, and you are ready for whatever comes next.

Front Stance

The front stance is a fully front-facing position. Your weight is about 70 percent on your lead leg and 30 percent on your rear leg. To find your front stance, begin in the ready position. Move your left foot forward a comfortable distance (approximately double shoulders' width), keeping your feet one shoulders' width apart and your hips facing forward (Figure 4-2). Bend your front leg, but keep the back leg relatively straight. You may want to let your back foot turn out slightly for comfort (Figure 4-3). A right front stance is performed with the right foot forward; a left front

Figure 4-1 *Ready position*

stance has the left foot forward. Your hands can rest in chambered position while you are practicing stances.

Figure 4-2 *Front stance. Feet should be a shoulders' width apart.* **Figure 4-3**

Beginners sometimes make the front stance too narrow (Figure 4-4). This leads to an off-balanced stance, like trying to stand on a balance beam. Maintain a shoulders' width between the outer edges of your feet for a good solid base. Another mistake sometimes made in the front stance is to turn the front foot at an angle. Wherever your foot faces, your body tends to follow. If you keep your front foot facing forward, your body will naturally want to face forward, as intended for the proper execution of this stance.

FRONT STANCE FORCE EXERCISE

The front stance is very strong from front to back and less strong from the sides, especially if your stance is too narrow. You can feel this for yourself by performing the following exercise with a partner.

Stand in a strong front stance. Have your partner push straight back on your shoulders. You should be able to resist well if you stay centered. Now, have your partner push on your shoulder from the side. If your stance is a shoulders' width apart, you will be able to resist somewhat, although not as firmly as when pushed from the front; if your stance is too narrow, you will not be able to withstand the force from the side and will tend to be knocked off balance.

A front stance is excellent for punching and for arm blocks. Frontal blocks and attacks are well supported in a front stance. Front kicks can be delivered well because your body is positioned perfectly for this technique. A full roundhouse kick is easily extended from front stance as well. A turning side kick can be extended from front stance, following a twist of the body, but the back kick is slow from a front stance. It requires a full rotation of the body to position yourself for a back kick. Other stances, such as horse stance and back stance, are better suited to back kick.

Figure 4-4 *Here the front stance is too narrow.*

Horse Stance

The horse stance is a side-facing position, similar to the position used in riding a horse. Turn sideways toward an imaginary opponent in front of you, and place your feet two shoulders' widths apart, parallel to each other, with your toes facing front. Bend your knees to a comfortable level (Figures 4-5 and 4-6). The stance should be solid but flexible, not too low, not too shallow. This permits movement through footwork, while anchoring the stance for blocks, counterattacks, or offensive moves. Your knees should be over your feet, not sagging to one side or the other. Your pelvis should be centered between your feet, so that weight distribution is under you and your hips are not leaning. Do not tilt your hips away, backward, or sideways from your center in the basic position. If a tilt takes place or is temporarily necessary, return your pelvis to the correct position as soon as you can, so it is under you and centered. The same goes for your head and shoulders. Always try to keep your body in line, which will keep your center of gravity sunk in the center of your body. This maintains balance and stability.

Figure 4-5 *Horse stance, front view*   **Figure 4-6** *Side view*

Turn only your head sideways to look sideways, this is the direction you will kick for side kicks and other techniques. For exercise drills in this stance, you can face forward to throw punches to the front, but don't use the horse stance for forward punches in sparring or self-defense; this position is weak from the front and the back.

EXERCISE FOR STRENGTH IN HORSE STANCE

Stand in a good horse stance and have your partner stand at your side and push on your shoulder. This stance is very strong and can resist a great deal of force from the sides. Next have your partner stand directly in front of you and push you back. You will find it difficult to resist a front push from horse stance. For this reason it is usually unwise to face an opponent in horse stance, but if you turn sideways, you will present to your opponent a strong narrow profile.

The horse stance is strongest side to side and is well suited for side kicks and whole body blocking, in which the hips are used to power blocks. As mentioned, the horse stance is stable and useful for resisting force from the side. Advanced forms, such as Ship Su, a black belt form, combine a 180-degree pivot with blocks to make them even more powerful.

Back Stance

The body profile for the back stance is in between the front stance's front-facing position and the horse stance's side-facing position. Place the ball of your front foot next to the heel of your back foot and continue to move it away from your center about two shoulders' widths. Keep your weight distribution sixty/forty, with more weight over the back leg. Some modern teachers turn the front foot forty-five degrees to the perpendicular, with toes facing forward (Figure 4-7).

In this stance, you will be in an excellent defensive position, since your weight is back, away from your opponent. This is one of the reasons that the back stance is the most commonly used stance in sparring. The back stance is useful for certain blocks and counterattacks, but not for others. It is a strong stance in most directions, while also being fairly mobile, allowing for the evasion needed in sparring.

The left back stance is performed with your left foot forward and more weight on your rear right foot. The right back stance has the right foot forward and extra weight over the back left leg.

Figure 4-7 *Back stance*

Cat Stance

The cat stance is part of traditional Chung Do Kwan as Won Kook Lee taught it; however, some later Chung Do Kwan teachers dropped it as a useful stance, because of its lack of stability. The cat stance can be a good transition stance for blocks and evasive footwork, but do not attempt to block strongly in the cat stance, because there is very poor anchoring in this stance.

Perform the cat stance by bringing one foot toward the other while turned sideways, toe touching the floor lightly. Ninety percent of your weight should be on the back foot (Figure 4-8). Your front foot is mobile and can quickly move forward to propel you into another stance. Your front leg is also in an excellent position to throw a quick front kick.

Figure 4-8 *Cat Stance*

Figure 4-9 *X-stance with downward X-block*

X-Stance

The cat and X-stances are the reverse of each other. If you spin out of a cat stance, you can be in an X-stance. The X-stance is used in intermediate to upper-level forms as a transition stance to jump into, to twist into and out of, and to advance into and out of. The X-stance can be used for defense, attacking, or counterattacking.

Place your front foot firmly on the floor. Cross your other foot behind it, with your weight on the ball of the back foot. Keep your knees close together.

Use the X-stance to step through and spin out of, for back kicks and hook punches, and also when grabbing. For example, in forms, the X-stance serves a number of different functions. In Pyong-An 4, the practitioner steps into an X-stance to execute an arm block. In Pyong-An 5, the practitioner jumps and spins to land in an X-stance, while performing a downward X-block (Figure 4-9). The black belt form, Yun Be, uses it extensively.

Another use of the X-stance is as a transition during cross-stepping. You can evade an attack by stepping back into an X-stance. This shorter step back puts you in an excellent position to quickly step back in for a counterattack. The mobility of this stance is a great advantage. In combination with blocks, attacks, and counterattacks, the X-stance makes it very difficult for an opponent to predict your next move.

Moving in Stance

Stance changes should be practiced and practiced, so they are smooth, controlled, and regular, not bouncing or rigidly awkward. It is important to practice relaxing and tensing with the correct rhythm and timing.

Begin with a left front stance (Figure 4-10). Place your two hands in chamber. Then, step forward with your right foot (Figure 4-11) into a right front stance. Maintain your foot position at a shoulders' width apart. Keep your center of gravity under you as you move (Figure 4-12). Move up the floor and then turn to move back. Try this exercise with the back stance, moving from left back stance to right back stance.

For the horse stance, begin in horse stance position. Next, bring your back foot across your front foot, forming an X-stance (Figure 4-13), and then, without stopping, step out into another horse stance (Figure 4-14). This kind of cross-stepping allows you to move in and out quickly. You will use this type of stepping for side kicks when performing basics.

Figure 4-10

Figure 4-11

Figure 4-12

Practice shifting from the X-stance into the cat stance by pivoting 180 degrees on both feet. Your legs will uncross, and you will find yourself in cat stance. Turn the other direction from the cat stance, and you will be back in the X-stance.

Figure 4-13   Figure 4-14

Stance Meditation

Awareness of your stance will help to enhance all your techniques. This meditation can be practiced at many points in a workout. Take a moment to pay
attention to your stance. You may find it helpful to briefly close your eyes.
Notice how your weight is distributed. Pay attention to how your feet are
placed. Adjust your stance if needed.

Standing in any stance position, slowly shift your weight from front to back
or side to side, until you are in the correct position for that particular stance.
Sense where your balance is firm and where it is off. Try this with each stance.
With practice, you can develop an inner sense for correct positioning.

Try moving from stance to stance with your attention on your balance.
Don't ignore the transitions. In motion and in stance, you can be in control of
your position.

A good stance forms a firm foundation for effective technique. Maintain
the correct stance while in motion. Practice in maintaining the correct stance
will help you gain the stability necessary to support tremendous power.

— 5 —

Power Punching

When Yi (a famous archer) taught people to shoot, he told them to pull the string on the bow its full length. The man who wants to cultivate himself must also develop himself to the full extent.

Mencius

A good punch is the cornerstone of any martial art. Learning how to punch hard, fast, and accurately will enhance your skills. Chung Do Kwan has developed techniques that bring everything together, mind and body working completely in harmony, to deliver dynamic, powerful punches.

The Fist

The punch begins and ends at the fist. How you make your fist affects the success of your punch. To form a fist, roll your fingers back tightly into your palm. Place your thumb across your fingers. Your thumb helps to keep your fist closed tightly (Figures 5-1, 5-2, and 5-3).

Figure 5-1

The largest knuckles are the striking point (Figure 5-4). In order to present these knuckles to the target, you have to align your fist. Place your knuckles on a target. Your fist should be aligned so that the force can travel straight back through your arm. Do not bend your wrist up, down, or side to side. If you punch with a bent wrist, the larger muscle groups won't support the force. Instead, the weaker wrist muscles will have to take up the force.

Figure 5-2

Figure 5-3

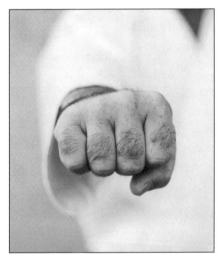

Figure 5-4

Punching Instructions

To learn punching, stand in a horse stance. Place your right hand in the chamber and place your left hand in an extended punch position, at middle target level (Figure 5-5). Move your chambered left fist out from your body. Pick a point in the air to aim for, and try to accurately strike there in the middle target range. This habit of aiming your punches will enhance your accuracy. Eventually you will be able to punch exactly at your intended target.

Extend your punch outward with fist fingers pointing upward until you are about seven inches from the target (Figure 5-6). Then twist your fist until the fingers face down and the punch is fully extended. This quick twist toward the end of your punch adds powerful torque to the movement (Figure 5-7).

Figure 5-5

Figure 5-6

Figure 5-7

As you are punching, pull back your right hand hard into the chamber with a force equal to the force of the punch, in order to balance your forward movement (Figure 5-8). The harder and faster you punch, the harder and faster you pull back. Time the pullback as if it were a simultaneous elbow strike to an opponent standing behind you. Every movement you make during training has many potential applications—even the supporting movements.

Figure 5-8 *Punching in front stance.*

Improving Your Punch: Body Alignment

Proper body alignment can add power to your technique. When you punch, you are extending your force outward from your arm; however, the most powerful punches utilize power from the entire body. In Chung Do Kwan, punches do not come just from the arm or shoulder. Real power is generated by using the chest, shoulders, and arms, supported by the latisimus dorsi muscles in the back. As you punch, tighten these muscle groups at the moment of contact. The alignment of fist, arm, and large muscles unifies your body for maximum power and also keeps you balanced. When students are slack in these muscle groups, their punches yank at the shoulder, often throwing the body alignment forward and twisting it. The straight punch moves toward the center, as the shoulders remain square. In this way, force generated by the large upper-body chest and back muscles can move smoothly out into the punch.

Since a punch is not generated from upper-body strength alone, a solid stance provides a firm foundation for any punch. The front stance is the strongest stance for a good punch. Review the previous chapter on stances for instructions. Remember that you are facing forward and that your weight is more forward than back, with your feet a shoulders' width apart. From this position, power can travel up from the floor and move into the punch.

The main power of Chung Do Kwan techniques comes from the center. The torso plays an important role in punching. The punch starts at the hip, the chamber. As you begin a right punch, rotate your hips with a countertwist back to add snap and focus from the center. You can manifest more power from the equal and opposite force created by correctly timed rotation of your trunk area while punching. (See chapter 3 for hip rotation instructions.)

Stomach muscles link the upper and lower body together, allowing movements to be unified. The upper body aligns with lower body best when the abdomen is a point of focus. Some students neglect this important area and because they do so their punches become one-dimensional, using only half of the body. Whenever you throw a punch, contract your stomach muscles as you near full extension. This allows the force from the floor to be transmitted up to your upper body and out into your punch, adding to the force from your upper body. Tensing the stomach muscles at the moment of impact also helps you to generate maximum power without becoming rigid.

Punch Focus Exercise

Stand in a front stance and extend your left punch with your right hand in the chamber. Close your eyes. Extend your right hand into a punch as you pull back your left. Move very slowly, keeping all your muscles relaxed without being lax. Then, at the end of the movement, tighten all the appropriate muscles: chest, arm, fist, back, stomach, and leg muscles. Hold that for a count of five, and then relax. Repeat this with the other hand. This exercise will help you to develop the ability to focus your muscles at the moment of impact. Also, your strength will increase because of the effect of dynamic tension as exercise for your muscles.

Punch Variation: Reverse Punch

The front punch is a strong attack from a medium distance. Chung Do Kwan also includes a punch called the reverse punch, which can be performed at close range. Standing in a right back stance, with your left foot back, punch with your left hand (Figure 5-9). The punch comes out across the body. This punch is called reverse punch because it is generated from the back hand over the rear foot, rather than from the front hand over the front foot, as in the front punch. The term reverse punch is used because the punch is delivered with the reverse hand to the lead foot, rather than the same hand as the lead foot. You can stand close to your target if you perform this punch in back stance. Using a little torque from the hips, twist toward the target, and then pull back to center again as you strike.

Practice your punches regularly and you will feel improvement over time. Each time you practice, try to do your very best. This is the secret to building powerful technique in Chung Do Kwan—and in everything you do in life. You will improve by doing it consistently. Punches can be performed as a part of your basics. See chapter 12 for instructions on how to include punches in your regular workout.

Figure 5-9

— 6 —

Thrusting Kicks

The wind moves, but the mind shakes the tree.

Korean Zen Master Chinul

Chung Do Kwan is famous for its forceful thrusting kicks. These techniques radiate penetrating, unstoppable power. This story illustrates the power of the Chung Do Kwan kick.

Grandmaster Son worked out early in the morning every day at Central Park in New York City. He usually wore street clothes so that he would not arouse attention. On a particular day, Son had just finished his workout and was starting to walk home. Four hoodlums saw this modest, unassuming man and thought he looked like an easy mark. They surrounded him and said threateningly, "Give us your money!"

Grandmaster Son looked at them calmly and smiled. "Oh, you are bad boys! Watch this," he said as he walked over to a huge oak tree. Without hesitation, he kicked it with a powerful side kick. The whole tree shook from the force. Realizing what the likely outcome would be, the four attackers turned and ran away as fast as they could, leaving Son to continue his quiet walk home.

Practitioners begin learning all the basic kicks early and continue to perfect them throughout the years. An excellent way to improve your kicks is to carefully and forcefully repeat them over and over. If you practice in this way, you will develop powerful techniques that are ready to use when you need them. Good form will bring about good function.

Front Kick

The front kick is the most straightforward kick to perform because it comes out directly from the front without any twists or turns. A front kick is usually practiced as a thrust in order to strengthen technique. A well-executed front kick is quick, balanced, and powerful. You can use this kick for lower-, middle-, and upper-target attacks.

One positive byproduct of the front kick is that as you work on raising your kick, you will become more flexible. We have had several students who began kicking only at knee height. With time and practice, much to their surprise, they were able to kick head height and higher! Properly performed, the back gets a good stretch, and the legs become more limber.

Executing the Front Kick

The front kick flows most naturally from a front stance. Your body faces front, with hips straight ahead. The striking point is the ball of the foot. The round-house kick also uses the ball of the foot as the striking point. The ball of the foot is hard with a small surface area that penetrates the target. To position your foot correctly, first point your toes and push your foot down, then pull your toes back. Notice how the ball of your foot tightens, making this part of your foot strong for striking. It is important to keep your toes pulled back to protect them from an opponent's block or from hitting them against the target accidentally.

Lift your back leg forward, bending your knee until your upper leg is beyond horizontal with the ground (Figure 6-1 and Figure 6-2). Then, thrust your leg outward to strike with the ball of your foot (Figure 6-3). Allow your upper body to come forward slightly as you kick, tightening your stomach muscles to unify your upper and lower body. Beginners often lean too far back, away from their kick. But this puts them off-balance. An observant opponent will take advantage of this mistake and throw the kicker over.

You can add extra power and extension to your front kick by thrusting your hips forward slightly as you kick. Beginners sometimes make the mistake of dropping their hips back as they kick, causing them to lose power and shorten the kick. Pushing your hips forward as the kick comes out adds an inch or two of reach and will also accelerate the speed and force of your kick.

Front kicks can be placed around defender's blocks. You can also use your front kick as a push kick at a middle target to stop an opponent from coming in too close or to push the opponent away. Front kicks also work well in combination with other kicks. A front kick followed by a turning side kick is one of the basic combinations practiced at every workout in Chung Do Kwan.

Figure 6-1   Figure 6-2   Figure 6-3

Side Kick

The side kick is one of Chung Do Kwan's most forceful and versatile kicks. Once you master this kick's thrusting power, you will be able to defend yourself with a single blow. With such a powerful kick, no second technique is necessary. One well-placed side kick overpowers the opponent, ending the encounter.

Executing a Side Kick

The side kick comes out from the side, so you will execute this kick by turning your side to face the target. Begin in a good horse stance, although you can perform the kick from other stances as well.

As you prepare to deliver the kick, draw your knee up toward your rib cage (Figure 6-4). The higher you draw your knee up, the straighter and deeper the thrust of the kick will be, and correspondingly, the more difficult to block. The supporting leg should be slightly bent. The heel of the supporting leg's foot lifts off the floor then drops to permit a slight pivot as you kick.

After your knee has been retracted, the kicking leg is extended rapidly out to the side. Because of the force that your foot must be able to endure when a target is contacted, the striking point is the heel or bottom of the foot, not the turned edge as in some lighter snap side kicks. Keep your foot parallel to the ground and flexed so that the heel strikes first, not the toes. A slight leaning of your upper body away from the target will take place naturally. Try not to lean back beyond approximately forty-five degrees (Figure 6-5).

Figure 6-4

Figure 6-5

The power center of the side kick is the waist and abdomen. Tense your abdomen in coordination with the kick, and exhale at the moment of focus. Your kicking leg should tense at the point of final extension, in coordination with your whole body, which sends force rebounding down to the ground and back up and out through your foot. Acceleration builds from the time the knee is raised until the final dynamic thrust outward of the leg. Let the same arm as the kicking leg swing back to counterbalance the kick, but try to keep the other hand up in front for blocking.

MOVING WITH THE SIDE KICK

You can extend the reach of your side kick by cross-stepping toward the target. Begin in a horse stance. Cross-step with your left foot in front of your right (Figure 6-6), then raise your right knee outward and extend the kick out sideways (Figure 6-7).

Figure 6-6

Figure 6-7

You can also perform the side kick from a front or back stance as a turning kick. Begin in front-stance position, raise your back leg with the knee coming up in front, as you would for the front kick. But as you come up, pivot forty-five degrees. With your body now turned sideways, you can thrust your side kick out toward a target in front of you.

POINTS TO REMEMBER

Several typical mistakes can easily be avoided with attention to certain details. Tense your foot and ankle at the point of focus. If your foot or ankle is loose, the force of the kick can hurt you!

Another common mistake made by beginners is to kick forward rather than sideways. This error can result from forward placement of the kick or misplacement of the hips. Do not drop your hip back. Your hips should line up directly with the kick and be aimed straight at the target.

Do not arch your back or crumple forward. Good posture with a twisting lean toward the target from the waist is best, tensing the abdomen.

ADVANTAGES OF THE SIDE KICK

Most people find it difficult to block a good side kick. The trajectory of the kick is a thrust straight in. This requires that the kick be evaded or deflected in order for it to be blocked successfully. Simply pushing it down won't work. The kick penetrates through a downward block.

The tremendous amount of force this kick can generate has many advantages. Competitors can use side kicks in tournaments to break through the opponent's defense for a point. In self-defense situations, most assailants are not prepared to successfully block this kick. If the opponent attempts to deflect the kick without being set firmly in a stance, or tries to take it on an arm, the side kick is likely to throw him over—end of encounter!

Roundhouse Kick

The principle of the circle has profound meaning in Eastern philosophy. The idea of infinite flow, ever-changing yet the same, gives it an elusive meaning. The roundhouse kick utilizes this principle. Unlike the side kick and front kick, which are both straight line attacks, the roundhouse kick is performed in a circle to sweep elusively around obstacles. A thrusting motion combined with circular momentum makes this a very powerful kick.

EXECUTING ROUNDHOUSE KICKS

A roundhouse kick can be performed with the back leg or the front leg. A roundhouse kick from the back leg comes around in a long sweeping motion. Stand in a front stance. Raise your back leg, bending at the knee, so that your lower leg is parallel to the floor (Figure 6-8). As you pivot on your standing foot, swing your hips around and arc your kicking leg in a 180-degree circle (Figure 6-9), as you straighten to hit with the ball of the foot. Similarly to the front kick, the foot should be extended with the toes pulled back and ankle correctly tensed; unlike the front kick, your foot is turned sideways, relatively parallel to the floor (Figure 6-10).

To complete the kick, bend your leg again and pull it back. This way, you maintain the balance and control necessary to move either forward or back following the kick. You will also lessen the chance for an opponent to trap your kick or throw you over.

The front roundhouse kick is the jab of leg techniques. This kick is extremely quick. Even though it has less power than the full roundhouse kick, it can surprise your opponent with its elusive trajectory.

Figure 6-8   Figure 6-9

Figure 6-10

Standing in back stance, lift your front leg with knee bent and foot held outward. Make a quick circular movement of the hips as you extend your leg. The ball of the foot is used for this kick, as in the full roundhouse kick.

POINTS TO REMEMBER

Your hips must be flexible for the roundhouse kick. General exercises that strengthen and limber the hips also help, such as leg scissors and side lifts from the ground. Stretch carefully before and after each workout. A good roundhouse kick should feel good at the hip, so don't permit excess tension to interfere with it. If your roundhouse kick feels uncomfortable or tight, you need to correct your technique.

Hip-Loosening Exercise

Stand in a horse stance with hands on your waist. Lift your left foot in an arcing motion across the front of your body as you pivot on your right foot. Place your foot down in a new horse stance, facing the opposite direction. As you swing your foot around, let your hip relax. You will feel a slight stretch when you do this exercise correctly. Don't force the motion. Repeat with the other foot, and then do several repetitions of the pattern.

Back Kick

The back kick can be an extremely strong kick. A back kick can be practiced first in a front stance. Lift your knee in front of you, and then kick out behind you. The bottom of the heel is the striking point in this kick. Be sure to look over the shoulder on the same side as the leg that is kicking so that you can place your kick where you want it; you will find that accuracy takes time to develop with this kick (Figure 6-11). Try pointing the heel of your supporting leg's foot toward the target first. This lines your body up correctly.

Figure 6-11

More commonly, this kick is performed by stepping into it. Begin in horse stance. Cross-step behind with your left foot and then raise your right knee, readying for a right back kick. In a continuously flowing motion, extend your kick out, striking with the heel. Keep your foot flexed, with the toes pointing downward as you strike.

Intermediate and Advanced Kicking

CRESCENT KICK

One kick used at the intermediate and advanced levels is the crescent kick. This kick is first introduced in the purple belt level forms, which is an intermediate level. The hip-stretching exercise for the roundhouse kick will also ready you for crescent kicks. Crescents get their name from the crescent arc made by the kick: a semicircular motion. There are two types of crescent kicks: inner and outer. The two crescent kicks arc in opposite directions. The striking point for the inner crescent kick is the inner arch toward the flat of the foot. The outer crescent strikes with the outside edge of the whole foot.

A kick can also be used as a block by advanced practitioners. Because legs are longer than arms, and because shoes will protect the blocker in self-defense situations, kicks can be very effective as blocks. Kicks can not only block an unarmed attack but can also be used to disarm an opponent holding a knife, short stick, or even a gun. Again, you should only attempt to disarm an opponent if you are highly advanced in your training.

Using kicks as blocks is a more advanced technique because it requires accuracy of placement to be effective. Good control is especially necessary if you are practicing with a partner, because these techniques can easily break bones. Aim carefully and touch lightly in training, not with full force.

Executing Crescent Kicks

Crescent kicks can be performed in a front stance, back stance, or horse stance. To perform an inner crescent, begin in front stance with your right foot back. Hold your left hand out straight in front of you, with your palm facing to the right as a target (Figure 6-12). Practicing with a target helps you to gain control and accuracy with this kick. Bring your back foot in an arcing motion around and across your body (Figure 6-13). Let your knee bend slightly. Lightly strike your hand with the instep of your foot. Keep your foot tight when you strike (Figure 6-14).

| Figure 6-12 | Figure 6-13 | Figure 6-14 |

Outer crescents can also begin in front stance. For this kick, raise your front foot and arc it away from your body outward in a crescent motion. Keep your knee slightly bent. Your foot should be flexed, with your toes pointing upward as you strike.

Advanced Variations of Basic Kicks

Practitioners should always keep improving their basic techniques. But advanced variations can be fun and help develop coordination and agility. Chung Do Kwan offers several variations on the basic kicks such as the reverse roundhouse, knee kick, and spinning back kick.

REVERSE ROUNDHOUSE KICK VARIATION

This technique can surprise an opponent because of its unexpected trajectory. Like the front roundhouse kick, this kick comes from the front leg. Standing in either a front or back stance, lift your front knee in front of you (Figure 6-15), then arc your foot out away from you to strike outward, with the ball of your foot twisted outward. A slight twist of the hips helps to snap this kick out. The striking point is the ball of the foot (Figure 6-16). Some hip mobility is required. If it hurts, don't do it.

Figure 6-15   Figure 6-16

KNEE KICK VARIATION

Knees can also be used in blocks and attacks at closer distances. The motions of the front kick and the roundhouse kick lend themselves to knee strikes and blocks. These techniques are middle-target strikes and blocks. They should not be used against hard bony areas but are more effective on softer, midsection targets such as the stomach or abdomen.

To perform the front knee technique, draw your knee up as you do for a front kick and strike with the area right below the knee. Strike with the top of the knee. Never use the kneecap as striking point for knee strikes: this is a fragile, unsuitable, vulnerable area that could be broken by using it. For a roundhouse knee, swing

Figure 6-17 *Roundhouse knee*

your leg around as if performing a roundhouse kick. The striking point for this technique is the upper thigh, near the knee (Figure 6-17).

SPINNING BACK KICK VARIATION

A variation of the back kick is the spinning back kick. Learning this kick is easier when you have a target to aim at, such as a heavy bag or a pad held by a training partner. Begin in back stance as you face your target. Step forward with your front foot. Follow this step with a half-turn with your other foot and a back kick at the target using the first foot. Look over your shoulder as you kick so that you can see the target as you strike. Retract your foot as you spin around to face front again. This kick requires a lot of practice to develop the flowing coordination and accuracy to consistently hit the target exactly where you want.

Flying Kicks

All of the basic kicks can be performed in the air. Some people are natural jumpers and will find that flying kicks come easily; others will have more difficulty performing a high-flying kick. However, everyone can benefit from practicing this technique: Flying kicks teach you to be springy and flexible in your technique. The ability to leave the ground and return again in control can be developed. The strength needed to spring up and kick builds elastic force and a tendency to instinctively find and recover balance—a great asset to any martial artist. Remember that in self-defense situations, flying kicks can be risky and should only be used sparingly. You cannot alter the trajectory easily, once committed. After you understand the principles of these kicks, and practice them carefully, you can develop safe and effective ways to use them.

EXECUTING FLYING KICKS

Flying kicks use the same kick dynamics as regular front kicks, side kicks, and roundhouse kicks. Practice flying kicks on a soft surface that is also firm enough for a balanced landing; a grassy area outdoors or mats indoors are ideal. For a flying front kick, begin by taking a few running steps to give you momentum. Taking off from one foot, raise both knees as you jump. At the height of your jump, extend one of your legs out for a front kick, then retract your foot so that you can land in a balanced stance. Either the foot used to push off or the opposite foot can be used for striking.

Flying side kicks can be very graceful, and side kicks lend themselves well to flying kicks. Take your running steps and then, as you jump, pivot ninety degrees in the air so that your side is facing the target (Figure 6-18). The higher you can raise your knees, the higher your kick will come out. Perform your flying side kick as you raise the other leg up, with your foot covering the groin area for protection against counterpunches (Figure 6-19).

Figure 6-18

Figure 6-19

A flying roundhouse kick is performed with a straight jump, as in the front kick, followed by the roundhouse kick (Figure 6-20). This kick is more challenging to perform as a flying kick because you must combine forward force with angular momentum. A jumping roundhouse, where you simply jump straight up without a running start, is easier to use for practicing this kick.

It is also possible to combine kicks, as in the double flying front kick—kicking with one leg after kicking with the other. A front kick followed by a roundhouse or side kick with the other foot also works well.

PERFECTING FLYING KICKS

You can improve the height of your flying kicks by jumping over a barrier that is progressively raised as you improve. We often have students practice jumping over a uniform belt loosely held by two people who gradually raise the belt with each jump. If a student jumps too low, one holder can let go of the belt so that the student can make a safe landing. Do not use rigid barriers as hurdles for practice.

Figure 6-20

You can also have a third person hold out a target pad, such as a clapper, for kicking. This helps you to train for accuracy with the flying kick. Perform flying kicks at a heavy bag for power training. You can learn to generate significant force in your flying kick by applying the usual basic principles to this technique: power, focus, accuracy, balance, speed, and correct relaxation. Target training of flying kicks can prepare you for a flying kick break.

– 7 –

Effective Blocking

When a force approaches
Take a strong stance
Await the correct moment
With an inward glance

C. Alexander Simpkins

You deflect offensive strikes from the opponent by using strong, focused blocks. The blocks in Chung Do Kwan can be so powerful that they break an opponent's arm but so controlled that they do not even produce a bruise on a training partner's arm. This is the power and precision of Chung Do Kwan in action. The principles are timeless and apply to many other arts, but Chung Do Kwan expresses the ultimate essence.

Types of Blocking

Blocks can be performed in two basic ways: with hands closed and with hands open. However, once blocking principles are fully understood, many variations become possible, such as blocks with the feet, and the use of strikes as blocks. But at first, hands and arms are the best way to block.

For consistent results, blocks to a punch or a hand strike are usually aimed just above the opponent's wrist. When blocking a kick, try to connect just above the ankle. If your block goes too high on the opponent's arm or leg you may get hit by the attack.

Closed-Handed Blocks

In Chung Do Kwan, closed-handed blocks are fundamental. Keeping your hands closed in a fist prevents the jamming of your fingers. The entire body is covered with four basic close-handed blocks: upward, downward, the double-arm block (from inside to outside) and the single-arm block, (from outside to inside). They can be performed to protect upper, middle, and lower targets.

Close-handed blocking offers a reliable, safe, and straightforward system to block in most situations. Once these basic blocks are mastered, you will always have a simple, stable set of blocks to cover any attack.

UPWARD BLOCK

Attacks to the upper-target areas are protected against with the upward block. To learn this block, begin in a right front stance with your right arm angled down in front of your body, fist closed, and left hand in the chamber (Figure 7-1). Sweep your hand upward, allowing your elbow to bend slightly so that the motion covers the front of your body. Your fist begins to rotate (Figure 7-2). Then, when you get near the top of your motion, allow your fist to pivot out so that your thumb ends up facing down when you finish the motion. This snapping motion at the end adds focus to the move (Figure 7-3).

Figure 7-1   Figure 7-2   Figure 7-3

When you understand the basic motion, try performing blocks in succession. Step into right front stance and and do a right upward block. Notice how the right upward block is performed over the right forward foot. Then as you step forward into a left front stance, perform another upward block with the left hand. The succession of techniques in motion are performed in basics (see chapter 12).

Middle-Target Blocks

Middle-target blocks are done in two ways, with a single-arm block and a double-arm block. These two blocks move the force away in opposite directions, so you have a way to cover the entire middle-target area against an attack coming at you from any angle.

The single-arm block, or "arm block," deflects the force from the outside and sends it across your body, out of the way. The single-arm block is performed by raising the blocking arm out to the side, bent at the elbow at a right angle, with your knuckles level with your head, facing toward you with your palm facing outward, fist closed (Figure 7-4). Swing your arm around across your body in a motion parallel to the floor (Figure 7-5). Rotate your fist around, stopping just a little past your centerline in front of your nose, tensing appropriately to focus, so that the attack is struck and deflected away, out of the line of attack (Figure 7-6). Usually performed in front stance, this block is a very strong defense that deflects the attacker's arm, and it can force him away from the target when performed with full force (Figure 7-6a).

Figure 7-4

Figure 7-5

Figure 7-6

Figure 7-6a

The double-arm block comes in from the opposite direction, from the inside of your body, deflecting outward. This block moves the incoming force away from your centerline to the outside. This block can be performed in the front stance as well as other stances; in the front stance, the full power can be expressed with hip motion and focus. The blocking point of the defender's arm is the inner wrist near the thumb and is applied with a twisting torque.

To perform the double-arm block, step into a left front stance as you swing both your arms to the right, and circle around toward the left (Figure 7-7) as you bring your left arm up to block, arm bent (Figure 7-8). Your right arm is placed lower, as a potential support. Your hands should be closed into fists. At the final moment of focus, your fist snaps around from facing down to facing inward, to add extra power (Figure 7-9). Coordinate this with a hip rotation as explained in chapter 3. The point of contact for the defender is the inner edge of the arm, just above the wrist (Figure 7-9a).

Figure 7-7

Figure 7-8

Figure 7-9

Figure 7-9a

LOWER-TARGET BLOCKS

The lower target is guarded by the downward block. This block is performed in a front stance, although downward blocks are performed in other stances, such as the back and horse stance, in more advanced forms. As you step into a left front stance, raise your left arm across your body (Figure 7-10) and sweep it downward (Figure 7-11) until you just barely pass your leg, several inches from your front knee. Your right hand should come back to the chamber to help balance the forces (Figure 7-12). The full sweep of this block can intercept an attack at any point and send it downward and out of the way. The point of contact is the outer edge of the arm, just above your wrist.

Figure 7-10

Figure 7-11

Figure 7-12

A variation of the downward block is used at the more advanced levels. This downward block moves from outside to inside. Start by holding your blocking arm, bent at the elbow, at shoulder level, held out, away from your centerline, and parallel to your side (Figure 7-13). The other arm should be extended on the opposite side and lowered. Bring the blocking arm arcing downward, using the inner edge of the arm as the blocking point. Place your other hand on your blocking arm, midway between the wrist and the elbow. Your fist will point up at the point of impact (Figure 7-14).

Figure 7-13

Figure 7-14

Open-Handed Blocks

Open-handed blocks, which include the knife-edge block, back-hand block, and palm-heel block, allow for additional angles and striking points. Blocking with the hand open also makes it easier to grab immediately after blocking and pull the opponent into a counterattack.

KNIFE-EDGE BLOCKS

Open-handed blocks that use the edge of the hand are known as knife-edge blocks. This is because of the sharp cutting action that this block makes. Knife-edge techniques, both the block and strike, are presumed to derive from knife and sword fighting. Keep in mind that the knife-edge block is a powerful and dynamic precision move. The block connects to the opponent's punch or kick with the edge of the hand. When well executed, this block stops the attack definitively and prevents further attacks by an opponent. But exactness in executing this block is essential.

Figure 7-15

Your knife-edge is located on the outside edge of your hand. To tighten this area, open your hand with your thumb placed tightly against your hand (Figure 7-15). Allow the ends of your fingers to curl slightly, and you will feel the muscles of your knife-edge tighten up. Try to keep your palm pulled flat and your wrist straight, so that your knife-edge becomes an extension of your entire arm.

To perform a knife-edge block, begin in left back stance with both hands open. The palm of the hand that is coordinated with the lead foot is facing up, while the palm coordinated with the rear foot is facing down (Figure 7-16). Bring both hands around in a half-circle in front of your body (Figure 7-17). The right hand should stop approximately three inches away from your body, near the center of your chest. The left hand should move out into the knife-edge position, with your arm bent at a forty-five degree angle and your fingertips just under the level of your eye so that you will not block your view (Figure 7-18). The motion of the knife-edge block is similar to the double-arm block, except that both hands are open and you are turned sideways in a back stance.

Figure 7-16   **Figure 7-17**   **Figure 7-18**

Certain fine points will help make this technique more effective. Keep your fingers tight and thumb in. Also, be sure that your palm faces out away from you, as it does when you wave hello to someone. This position best presents your knife-edge to the attacker (Figure 7-18a).

Figure 7-18a

Knife-edges can give a sharp, painful block to the opponent. In training, the backhand can be used so that you can master the timing, distance, and accuracy without hurting your opponent. In self-defense, just turn the edge outward; then you get "the cutting edge." (See chapter 13 on self-defense.)

Knife-edge blocks may be performed inward or outward. The edge of the palm is the striking point to the target of the opponent's arm, wrist, or leg. The knife-edge can be used on all target areas.

PALM-HEEL BLOCKS

The open palm is a strong area for blocking as well as striking. However, these blocks are more advanced, requiring pinpoint accuracy. Keep your fingers pulled back hard and your hand bent back at the wrist (Figure 7-19). With time, your wrist will become more flexible to allow for a more exposed palm heel.

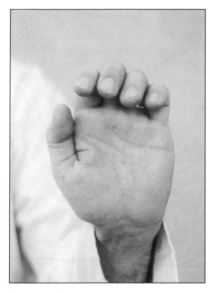

Figure 7-19

Figure 7-20

Palm-heel blocks can be performed up to down, down to up, and outside to inside or inside to outside. To deflect middle-target attacks, swing your arm around in an arc, starting from outside and moving in to the center. Downward palm-heel blocks begin from above and arc down. Upward palm-heels arc down to up. Advanced forms combine double palm-heel blocks, one coming down as the other comes up, to deflect double punches (Figure 7-20).

Toughening

A block is only as strong as the blocking instrument. Therefore, you will benefit from toughening your blocking areas. Toughening should be done carefully and gradually to build up strength without injury. Injuries will slow you down, so don't be overzealous!

TOUGHENING ON YOUR OWN

You can use a plastic baseball bat or a padded stick to condition your arms and legs. Strike lightly, five or six times, to the blocking areas inside the arm, outside the arm, and on the back of the arm, just above your wrist. You can also toughen your shins, sides, and the backs of your legs to help you be able to take a block on your leg. Do this a small number of times each day or every few days, and gradually increase the intensity and number of strikes, as you are able. You should not produce any bruising. Over a number of months, you will become tougher. Be patient. You can use traditional liniments for comfort during this conditioning process; these are available from oriental herb stores and martial arts suppliers.

PARTNERED TOUGHENING EXERCISE

You can work with a friend to toughen each other at the same time. Start out gently, and gradually increase your force as both partners become conditioned and able to handle the exercise comfortably and safely.

Face your partner in a front stance. Bring your right arms up to block each other on the inner edge of your arms, then swing your arms down into a downward block to block the outer edge of your arms. Repeat up to ten times, and then switch arms (Figure 7-21 and Figure 7-22). Use only enough force to condition each other. Do not cause bruising. Conditioning is achieved gradually over a long time and will not be accelerated by unnecessary roughness.

Figure 7-21

Figure 7-22

Next, bring your arm up to perform single-arm blocks toward each other, striking the outer edge of your arms together (Figure 7-23). You can also do this exercise with knife-edge blocks, striking each other at your knife-edges, but again, do not hurt each other.

Figure 7-23

Advanced Blocking Techniques

Crescent kicks make effective blocks against a punch, another kick, or an attacker holding a weapon such as a knife. Bring your leg around to strike just above the wrist, in the case of a punch, or above the ankle, in the case of a kick. If you are wearing shoes, a crescent block against a weapon hand may disarm the opponent; however, this should only be tried once you've reached very advanced levels of training.

Other kicks can also be used as blocks: A front kick can come up under an attack to knock it away in an upward direction. A roundhouse kick can be used to push the attack over toward the side. Side kicks can also be used to deflect an attack.

Timing is crucial in kick blocks. They are usually reserved for more advanced practitioners because they have to be quick and accurate to be effective. Practice in the three-step to develop your skills with these blocks.

— 8 —

Dynamic Strikes

First of all, keep martial arts on your mind, and work
diligently in a straightforward manner; then you can
win with your hands . . .

Musashi

Chung Do Kwan utilizes many parts of the hands and arms for striking. You
may be surprised at how many good striking areas you have available to you.

Hands can be open or closed. Different parts of the hand can be used in
each of these positions. For open hands use the edge of the hand and the palms.
Strikes with the knuckles and the bottom of the fist are performed with closed
hands. Other parts of the arm, such as the elbow, are used in varying types of
elbow strikes.

Knife-Edge Strike

Chung Do Kwan uses one of the most powerful techniques in martial arts; it is
known as the "knife-edge strike." Like knife-edge blocks, this technique gets its
name from its open-handed cutting action. When performed successfully, the
knife-edge strike slices at the target with a sharp, penetrating blow, the result of
narrowing the striking point to a thin edge.

The knife-edge strike is performed in a back stance. To execute a left-handed
knife-edge strike, bend your left arm across your body, up at the level of your neck,
as you bring your right hand around at chest height. Note that your hand is tilt-
ed, with your knife-edge facing the floor so that it can snap around at the end of
the strike. Your arms will be crossed in front of your body. This X-block position
sets up a strong defense to begin your movement (Figure 8-1).

Swing your left hand around in an arc, palm up, parallel to the ground for
the strike (Figure 8-2). This strike uses circular rotation of the arms for added
power. Keep your arms and both shoulders on the same plane, aligned in a
straight line. Just before you complete the strike, snap your hand around into

position so that your palm faces downward, thumb drawn tightly to the hand, knife-edge facing outward. This final snap at the end of the move adds extra whipping power to the attack.

Figure 8-1

Figure 8-2

Figure 8-3

Finish the movement with your knife-edge facing outward and your arm extended from the shoulder toward your target, which could be the side of an opponent's neck. At the same time, bring your right hand around into the chamber. Keep your weight back in the back stance, even though you are expressing your force outward with the strike. In this way you remain protected, out of the range of an opponent's counterstrike. Maintain control by pulling your other hand back hard into the chamber as you maintain your back stance (Figure 8-3).

APPLICATION OF THE KNIFE-EDGE STRIKE

The slicing action of the knife-edge strike is especially suited to slipping in around a defense. The recipient of a properly focused knife-edge will often feel a sharp, digging pain from the strike.

Knife-edge strikes are usually performed at a middle distance. Knife-edge attacks can be aimed horizontally at lower, middle, and upper targets. The knife-edge can also be performed vertically, downward or upward, as well. The knife-edge block motion can also be used as a strike to knock a weapon out of the hand of an assailant. Again, this should only be attempted if you are very advanced in this technique.

Palm-Heel Strikes

In Chung Do Kwan, the palm-heel area is used for strong swinging strikes and blocks. Use of the palm area is drawn from the movements of tigers; the heel of the palm resembles the paw of a tiger

The palm striking point is located on the large fleshy area on your palm. If you turn your hand palm-up and tighten your hand as in a knife-edge strike, you will notice that the area below your thumb gets tight, too. Now bend your hand back at the wrist so that your palm is exposed. Curl your fingers and pull them back, while keeping the knuckles extended. Whenever you perform the palm strike, you must be sure to keep your fingers out of the way so that they do not hit first. The base of the palm is more protected than other areas, making it a good striking point. (See Figure 7-19.)

Palm strikes are performed from several different directions. Begin with your hand in chamber position. Extend your arm out as in the front punch. Position your hand for a palm strike, fingers up with your hand open, wrist bent back, and palm facing forward. The palm is the striking point, so be sure to keep your fingers pulled back. As you strike, pull your other hand back to give you additional push-pull force, similar to punching. Aim to middle or upper targets (Figure 8-4 and Figure 8-5).

A more advanced palm strike begins with your arm at your side with your palm facing forward. Bring your palm up in an arcing motion to upper target level for a strike under the chin of an opponent. You can also swing your arm around from the side, to perform a side palm strike. These strikes require accuracy to be effective. Advanced practitioners will possess the precision of placement that these strikes require, but beginners should stick with the basic palm strike.

Figure 8-4

Figure 8-5

These movements are often practiced using dynamic tension. You tighten your muscles hard to resist the opposing muscles as you move your arm in the palm strike arc. In an advanced form, Ship Su, performed at black-belt level, one arm moves down as the other arm moves up (Figure 8-6). This form helps to build the muscles needed for strong, dynamic palm strikes and blocks.

Figure 8-6

Beginners should practice palm strikes on a pad or kwon go to help toughen the palm area and learn the movement. Once your palm area is strong, you can use it as another option for punching.

Elbow Strikes

The elbow is another section of the body that makes an excellent striking weapon. It offers special qualities of body dynamics and distance variation to surprise and overwhelm an opponent.

The striking point for strong elbow techniques is not the tip of the elbow—the tip is fragile and should not be used forcefully against hard surfaces, though it can be used for raking motions. A better striking point that can be toughened for strong, forceful use is located two inches or so from the elbow, on the outside edge of the arm, either below or above the elbow tip, depending upon the direction of elbow strike: forward, backward, or downward.

Elbow strikes can be done from two positions of the arm. In the first type, the arm begins bent and held parallel to the ground. The striking motion can be performed by moving from outward to inward, striking downward or upward in an arc. Also, these kinds of strikes use the point below the elbow tip for striking. Both approaches appear in many Chung Do Kwan forms. In the second position, the arm is bent and held so the arm is perpendicular to the ground. These strikes may swing up or down and can use the area above the elbow tip as the striking point. Elbow strikes can also be done by combining these two motions, as in a downward elbow strike that arcs around from position one and uses the striking point below the elbow. This is a very powerful strike, often used for breaking solid materials such as wood, tiles, bricks, or cement.

Inward elbow strikes require the coordination of the whole body in order to deliver full power. To practice, begin in a solid right front stance. Next, extend your right hand and arm, with fingers pressed together and thumb pressed against the hand. Hold your left arm, bent at the elbow, parallel to the floor, with fist tight, drawn behind your shoulder line, similar to the chamber position for a punch (Figure 8-7). Finally, swing the striking elbow around to the target, tensing your stomach muscles, and allow your hip to pivot toward the target (Figure 8-8 and Figure 8-9). Do not hit your hand with full force, just use it for aim. Focus your upper body muscles as you finish the movement.

Figure 8-7

Figure 8-8

Figure 8-9

Outward elbow strikes are performed with a sweeping motion away from the centerline. Begin in a horse stance with your right arm raised and bent, held at shoulder height, parallel to the floor. Your fist should be directly in front of your centerline at the chest (Figure 8-10). Move your elbow outward in an arcing motion toward an imaginary target to the side and slightly behind you (Figure 8-11).

Distance is broken down into ranges. You can think of kicks as long-range techniques, while punches and knife-edge strikes are medium range ones. Elbow strikes are performed at short range. It is important to learn to gauge your distance for elbow techniques. Stand close to a heavy bag or have a partner hold a striking target pad for you. Bend your arm in the elbow position and swing toward the target. You should be close enough to penetrate the target. This practice will also help to strengthen your elbow area. Apply good focus at the moment of impact. You can toughen this area to make it strong enough to withstand the force you will learn to generate.

Figure 8-10

Figure 8-11

Back-Fist and Bottom-Fist Strikes

Different areas of the fist are also used for striking. The back-fist strike uses the knuckles, as in the forward punch, but does so in a sweeping arc. Perform this technique by moving your fist around in a circle across your body and out. The wrist can be bent back to expose a larger area of knuckles to the target. Intermediate practitioners perform this movement in a back stance and an X-stance in their forms (Figure 8-12). The advantage of this technique is the unusual angle of entry, which can be difficult for the opponent to block.

Figure 8-12

The bottom-fist is a powerhouse strike, which can be used for breaking. The bottom area of the fist is naturally strong. If you clench your fist hard, this area becomes protectively tight. The bottom-fist can be performed as a downward strike. Stand in a front stance and raise your fist above your head and slightly behind it (Figure 8-13). Sweep downward in front of your body. As you do, bring your other hand back into the chamber to balance the force (Figure 8-14). You can practice this strike on a kwon go. Use one specially prepared for this, attached to a low stand. Strike to the center of the pad. Let your stance drop low as you strike, keeping your front leg bent and back leg straight. Do not lean forward at the waist beyond 45 degrees when you drop; simply lower your center of gravity. Done correctly, this strike utilizes the whole body to add power for a dynamic breaking technique.

Figure 8-13

Figure 8-14

All of these hand strikes need to be practiced to be perfected. You can perform them as strikes in the air to develop correct form, balance, and speed. Power can be built by striking a surface such as a pad, body shield, heavy bag, or kwon go. All of these striking areas need to be properly toughened in order to be useful. Your technique is only as strong as your body can handle.

~ PART III ~

Expressing Power in Motion

~ 9 ~

Forms

Pattern is the power of beauty.

Yanagi

Chung Do Kwan uses forms as an important tool for learning—as a means to express focused power in controlled action. Like classical literature, forms are the collective heritage of the art, with levels of meaning hidden within. Just as literature holds deep insights, forms encode many levels of understanding within the movements. The patterned movements are handed down, teacher to student, with exactness, according to the tradition, to pass along the spirit of Chung Do Kwan.

There is a correct way to do each form, but precision does not mean there is no room for individual differences. Classical form must be interpreted. Every *body* is a little different, and Chung Do Kwan is for everybody. Anyone can master the forms if he or she tries hard enough.

Each belt level, from beginner to advanced, has several forms, with lessons appropriate to that level. Forms also help instructors to assess the student's readiness to progress to the next level. As students develop their precision and control, they become capable of performing progressively more difficult movements in higher belt forms.

Simply being able to get through the pattern of movements is only the first step to mastery. Every move of every form should be executed with the six basic qualities of movement discussed in chapter 3: power, speed, accuracy, focus, balance, and relaxation. Forms give students the opportunity to perfect their techniques according to these principles. Original Chung Do Kwan forms include the Pyong An, a series of five forms; three Chul Gi forms; Pal Sek; Ship Su; Yun Bee; and Jion. The different forms emphasize specific skills. Some forms are muscle forms, which build focus, strength, and power. Others work more on balance, agility, and speed. All of these qualities are important in building a good martial artist. Use forms to improve concentration, train in precision movement, and develop intensity.

These forms are very ancient and are drawn from Okinawan and the earlier Chinese forms. Variations of these forms are still practiced in Chinese, Okinawan, and Japanese styles. But the way Chung Do Kwan forms are done is unique to this style and expresses its deeper spirit.

Some of the Chung Do Kwan masters have made modifications of Won Kook Lee's original forms. Other modern Chung Do Kwan schools have incorporated newer Korean forms, following the path toward modernization that Tae Kwon Do has taken in Korea.

We present a selection from the original Chung Do Kwan forms. The newer forms are readily available in books on Tae Kwon Do *hyungs* (forms), but the traditional forms are harder to find. Tae Kwon Do practitioners from all styles may enjoy exploring their roots by practicing these older forms.

Our teacher, Grandmaster Son, created two beginner forms to carefully guide the beginner into the style: Kuk Mu 1 and Kuk Mu 2. These forms teach a simple shift from a back stance to a front stance, block to strike. At the yellow belt level, students learn an expanded version of Pyong An 1, which prepares the student for the more complex moves in Pyong An 2. Other masters under Grandmaster Son added three more Kuk Mu's to be performed at middle levels.

Beginner Forms

PYONG AN I

We will begin with a simple version of Pyong An 1, drawn from the early practice of Chung Do Kwan. Instructions for this simple version of Pyong An 1 are included here to give you a firm foundation. The beginner is taught his or her first forms as a literal set of blocks and punches. The basic form makes an "I" pattern. The sides are symmetrical to the front. Foot patterns are rhythmic; the stance is in the basic front stance. The four points of the compass are covered, north, south, east, and west, to simulate defending against four attackers from all sides. The differences between a block and a punch, and defense and attack, are defined. Positioning in defense and offense is practiced. Students learn how to shift stances and position, turning and stepping to meet attackers from all four sides. Through this form, beginners take their first steps on the path of discovery.

Begin in the ready position with feet a shoulders' width apart, fists facing each other at the level of your belt (see Figure 4-1 for a review of the ready position). Raise your left arm, bent at the elbow, and perform a downward block as you step into a left front stance, ninety degrees to the left (Figure 9-1). Your right hand should move simultaneously into the chamber position. Step forward into a right front stance as you perform a punch with your right hand and chamber with the left (Figure 9-2).

Pivot in a clockwise direction, 180 degrees as you step with the right foot into a right front stance and perform a right downward block (Figure 9-3). Then, step forward into a left front stance as you throw a left punch (Figure 9-4). You have now effectively dealt with an attacker on your left side and then one on the right side.

Next, step forward toward the front with your left foot into a left front stance as you perform a left downward block (Figure 9-5). Then, perform three consecutive punches, right (Figure 9-6), left (Figure 9-7), right (Figure 9-8), as you step forward into a right, left, and then right front stance with each punch.

Now, you will repeat the pattern in the opposite direction. Begin with a 270-degree clockwise turn to the left (Figure 9-9) as you perform a left downward block in left front stance (Figure 9-10). Follow with a right punch in right front stance (Figure 9-11). Turn 180 degrees to the right, and perform a right downward block (Figure 9-12) and left punch in front stances (Figure 9-13). Then turn ninety degrees to face the back and perform a left downward block (Figure 9-14) followed by three punches (right, left, right) in front stances.

For the final section of the form, turn 270 degrees to repeat the first four moves of the form: left downward block, right punch, clockwise turn 180 degrees to a right downward block, and left punch. Finally, return to the ready position. You should be standing exactly where you started.

Figure 9-1

Figure 9-2

Figure 9-3

Figure 9-4

Figure 9-5

Figure 9-6

Figure 9-7

Figure 9-8

Figure 9-9

Figure 9-10

Figure 9-11

Figure 9-12   Figure 9-13   Figure 9-14

LESSONS FROM PYONG AN 1

This basic form helps the new student learn how to move from one position to another, from a block to a strike. Figure 9-14a shows the downward block in this form deflecting a front kick. Once the kick is effectively blocked, the defender can move in for a punch, as in the form. Shifts in direction are also introduced so that the student can be ready to defend against multiple attackers. This form builds a foundation to ready the student for the more complex teachings that are to follow, which we will describe later in this chapter.

Figure 9-14a *This block can be used very effectively to block a lower target front kick. Also see Figure 9-1.*

Intermediate Forms

Pyong An 2

Pyong An 2 is taught at the yellow belt through green belt levels. The pattern for this form is much more complex than that of the beginner form. Different angles of blocking and attacking are introduced. This form also is the first to present varying levels of difficulty in movements. To master this form, you need to isolate the harder moves and practice them separately. Then, they can be integrated back into the sequence for a smooth performance.

Begin in the ready stance. Turn ninety degrees to the left as you step out with your left foot into a left back stance. Perform two blocks at the same time: a right upward block and a left rising block to the rear. The tops of the left knuckles should align with the top of the right fist (Figure 9-15). Next circle around for a right uppercut as the left hand is drawn in (Figure 9-16). Finally, still in a left back stance, perform a left punch straight out to the left as your right hand pulls back into the chamber position (Figure 9-17).

Next repeat these three movements to the other side, as shown by Figures 9-18, 9-19, and 9-20. Shift into a right back stance and perform the double blocks: left upward block and right rising block. Then, do a left uppercut, followed by a right punch.

Next is a balance move: From the previous right back stance, draw your right knee up high, close to the left leg, as you draw your left hand into the chamber and place your right fist on top of your left one (Figure 9-21). Face toward the rear and perform a simultaneous side kick and punch to the rear (Figure 9-22 and Figure 9-22a). Take extra care to perform these attacks with precision and good balance. Keeping your balance, bring your right foot down into a left back stance, facing the front with your hands in the left knife-edge block position (Figure 9-23). Then, perform two more knife-edge blocks: right (Figure 9-24) followed by left (Figure 9-25) in back stances, stepping forward with each block. For the final technique of this series, step into a deep right front stance as you perform a spear-hand thrust to the diaphragm with the right hand (Figure 9-26 and Figure 9-26a), and "yutz!"

Turn in a counterclockwise direction 270 degrees so that you face at a 45-degree angle toward the back, and perform a left knife-edge block in a left back stance (Figure 9-27). Follow this with a right knife-edge in right back stance along the same line (Figure 9-28). Step out 90 degrees with your right foot into right back stance as you perform a right knife-edge block (Figure 9-29), followed by a left knife-edge block in left back stance (Figure 9-30).

This next series is performed facing toward the back but is pictured from the front so you can see the details of the techniques. Pivoting on the right foot, turn 180 degrees to the left as you bring your left foot around in an arc into a right front stance. Your right arm swings down around for a back arm block (Figure 9-31) and continues to flow around up into a bent-arm block position. Your left hand pulls back into the chamber, and your head turns to face your blocking arm. This circular sweep is one continuous movement (Figure 9-31a). Next, pivot toward the back as you perform a front kick with the back left foot (Figure 9-32) followed by a reverse punch with the left arm (Figure 9-33).

Next, you will repeat the pattern on the other side. Bring the left foot over and turn to the right, into a right front stance, as you perform the sweeping circular block from down to up with your left hand (Figure 9-34). Then, follow this with a right front kick (Figure 9-35) and right reverse punch (Figure 9-36). The series ends with a step forward into tight front stance, as you perform a right double-arm block (Figure 9-37 and 9-37a) and "yutz!"

For the final series of the form, turn 270 degrees to the left, into a left front stance, facing forward again, as you perform a left downward block (Figure 9-38). Follow this with a left open-handed upward block, without moving your feet (Figure 9-39). Then, step forward into right front stance and perform a right upward block with fist closed (Figure 9-40). Then, repeat the pattern on the other side. Step ninety degrees to the right, into right front stance, as you perform a right downward block (Figure 9-41), followed by a right open-handed upward block (Figure 9-42). Then, step forward into a left front stance as you perform a left upward block (Figure 9-43).

Figure 9-15   Figure 9-16   Figure 9-17

Figure 9-18   Figure 9-19

Figure 9-20

Figure 9-21

Figure 9-22

Figure 9-22a

Figure 9-23

Figure 9-24

Figure 9-25

Figure 9-26

Figure 9-26a

Figure 9-27

Figure 9-28

Figure 9-29

Figure 9-30

Figure 9-31   **Figure 9-31a**

These two moves are performed facing the back.

Figure 9-32   **Figure 9-33**   **Figure 9-34**

These three moves are performed facing the back.

Figure 9-35

Figure 9-36

Figure 9-37 *This move is performed facing the back.*

Figure 9-37a

Figure 9-38

Figure 9--39

Figure 9-40

Figure 9-41

Figure 9-42

Figure 9-43

Lessons from Pyong An 2

The four knife-edge moves have introduced blocking at a forty-five-degree angle to the attack. Beginners learn how to completely avoid an attack by stepping directly back. In Pyong An 2, you perform subtler blocking at forty-five-degree angles to the attack that use leverage to your advantage.

Figure 9-44

Figure 9-45 *The defender blocks at an angle to the side kick and then uses this to her advantage to throw the attacker off balance.*

This form also teaches you how to shift your angles from block to strike. The sweeping circular block can be interpreted as a defense against a kick; here it is a defense against the kick and punch that is performed in the next two moves of the form. You learn how to quickly and efficiently turn ninety degrees to an incoming front kick to avoid it (Figure 9-44) and block with a pushing back arm block (Figure 9-45), followed by the arm block to a kick. Then, it requires only a simple turn to perform a counter front kick and reverse punch.

Pyong An 4

Pyong An 4 is one of the advanced-level forms, taught at purple belt. Begin in the ready position, similarly to the previous forms. Step out to the left into a left back stance as you simultaneously perform an open-handed upward block with your right hand and a sideways open-handed block with your left hand (Figure 9-46). Your body faces front as your head turns to the left to look at your blocks. The fingertips of your left hand should be aligned with the fingertips of your right hand. Next, move your right foot back as you bring your hands across your body for a smooth and powerful transition from position 1 to position 2, turning 180 degrees to the right to perform a right back stance and the same double blocks on the other side (Figure 9-47).

Figure 9-46

Figure 9-47

The next position is a lower X-block in a left front stance, to block (Figure 9-48). Then, move forward into a right double-arm block in a right front stance (Figure 9-49).

Figure 9-48   Figure 9-49

The next series will require extra practice to perfect. Ready yourself for the next move by drawing your left hand into the chamber and placing your right fist vertically on top as you raise your left knee (Figure 9-50). Then, perform a punch with your left hand, and at the same time throw a left side kick (Figure 9-51). Bring your kicking leg down into a left front stance, turning ninety degrees to the left as you perform a right elbow strike (Figure 9-52). Bring your right open hand around for the target. Next, face ninety degrees to the front as you move into a back stance (Figure 9-53). Place your right fist into the chamber and your left fist vertically on top as you raise your right knee (Figure 9-54) and perform the simultaneous punch/kick combination with your right hand and foot (Figure 9-55), followed by a left elbow strike to the right side (Figure 9-56).

Figure 9-50

Figure 9-51

Figure 9-52

Figure 9-53

Figure 9-54

Figure 9-55

Figure 9-56

From this position, pivot ninety degrees toward the front without moving your feet, and rotate your body an extra forty-five degrees as you perform an upward knife-edge block with your left hand and a simultaneous open-handed knife-edge strike to neck level with your right hand (Figure 9-57). From this position, throw a right front kick directly in front of you (Figure 9-58), and then leap forward into a right X-stance while your right hand does a back-fist strike to the face and your left hand moves into the chamber (Figure 9-59); yell "yutz!"

Next perform a 270-degree counterclockwise turn toward the back and step into a left front stance. Extend both hands out as if grabbing the collar or lapels of a jacket, twisting and pulling down slightly for a secure grip (Figure 9-60 and Figure 9-60a). All the moves in the series that follows are performed facing the back, but are pictured here facing front for better visibility. Pull your hands down as you throw a right front kick, simulating pulling the opponent into your kick (Figure 9-61). Then, immediately follow with a right and then left middle-target punch, as you step into right front stance (Figure 9-62 and Figure 9-63). Leave the second punch extended as you bring your left fist back into the chamber. Then step ninety degrees to the right into a right front stance and repeat the pattern on the other side: grab (Figure 9-64 and Figure 9-65), left front kick (Figure 9-66), and left punch, right punch in a left front stance (Figure 9-67 and Figure 9-68).

Figure 9-57   Figure 9-58   Figure 9-59

Figure 9-60   Figure 9-60a

Figure 9-61   **Figure 9-62**   **Figure 9-63**

These three moves are performed facing the back.

Figure 9-64   **Figure 9-65**   **Figure 9-66**

Figure 9-67   **Figure 9-68**

These two moves are performed facing the back.

Still facing toward the back, step forty-five degrees back to the center with your left foot as you perform a left double-arm block (Figure 9-69). Then, step forward into a right front stance and perform two more double-arm blocks, advancing in a straight line: a right double-arm block in a right front stance (Figure 9-70), and then forward again into left front stance for another left double-arm block (Figure 9-71).

Without moving your feet, bring your open hands up, extended at arms length to head-height position, as if grabbing an opponent at the back of the head (Figure 9-72 and Figure 9-72a). Then, pull your hands sharply down as you raise your right knee up between your hands (Figure 9-73) and yell "yutz!" Immediately pivot 270 degrees on your left foot and drop into left back stance, now facing front, as you perform a left knife-edge block (Figure 9-74). You should be facing at a forty-five-degree angle. Then, step ninety degrees to the right, into a right back stance, and perform a right knife-edge block (Figure 9-75). On command, bring your right foot back to the ready position to end the form.

Figure 9-69

Figure 9-70

Figure 9-71

Figure 9-72

Figure 9-72a

All of these moves (Figures 9-69 through 9-72a) are performed facing the back.

Figure 9-73 *Performed facing the back.*

Figure 9-74

Figure 9-75

Lessons from Pyong An 4

This form offers many new techniques that have useful self-defense applications. For example, pulling the opponent into your front kick not only adds greater power to the kick but also prevents the opponent from escaping your kick. The elbow strike also captures the opponent with the other hand to make the strike more powerful (Figure 9-76). Double-handed blocks allow you to defend against a much stronger opponent. A simultaneous block and strike will make the strike more likely to connect (Figure 9-77). All of these skills can be very useful in self-defense situation.

Forms as Moving Meditation

The mind is very important for mastering forms. You will reach a higher level of performance when you can empty your mind of all thought and simply perform the form without any distraction.

Forms teach you moving meditation. To do a form well you develop the martial arts discipline of focusing attention fully on what you are doing. What seems confining to the novice is the ultimate freedom to the master. The pattern is only an apparent boundary. Actually, forms can set you free to concentrate fully, focusing on precision, speed, and strength, to orient yourself deliberately in space with decisive motions. Black belts often find that the practice of forms is enlightening.

Figure 9-76

Figure 9-77

Forms at any level improve as the ability to focus your mind is intensified. Begin this exercise by doing a form you would like to improve. After you have completed the form, close your eyes. Relax your muscles wherever they may be unnecessarily contracted, and breathe calmly. Try paying close attention to your breathing sensations, as you inhale and exhale. Now, using your imagination, perform the form in your mind. Do not move. Imagine that you are able to perform with maximum intensity, focus, precision, balance, and speed, without being overly tense. Try to vividly feel the motions as you imagine this. Now, open your eyes. Execute the form at your very best. Most students will experience an improvement. Experiment with modifications that help.

Using Forms to Expand Your Understanding

Some martial artists do not use forms as part of their training. They believe that classical forms practice leads to rigid responses and causes stale reactions. Instead, they practice combinations of moves with a definite practical application. This objection can be addressed by how you approach your forms. Looked at with a flexible frame of reference, forms can open the door to many possibilities.

Practitioners learn best when they truly grasp the inner nature of the form, which is not limited to an overt definition of the movements. Give yourself space for insight to grow and evolve. The boundaries of the form become parameters within which to learn. The precise and exacting performance of classical forms permits this development to take place. Forms interpretation requires an open, searching perspective.

Forms are wellsprings of meaning, valuable to anyone who is willing to delve into them to search for what the forms have to offer. Like a selection of good literature, forms contain many possible interpretations just waiting to be discovered. The level of meaning that can be found in the forms is limited only by the practitioner's level of understanding. In time, you will grow in your capacity to comprehend at a deeper level.

At first, to the novice, forms may seem to lack practical applications. They seem more of a dance art than a martial art. But the paradox of forms is that they permit complex learning far beyond what is apparent on the surface. To get to the more complex levels, however, the door to those teachings must be entered and the threshold crossed. Direct interpretation of the moves is only the beginning stage of understanding.

Finding the Hidden Moves in Forms

We can look at the beginning forms as examples of the multilevel applications and multiple meanings that are hidden within forms in a general sense. We encourage you to analyze all the forms presented here, along with the forms you already practice. You will be surprised to find a wellspring of advanced techniques already well on their way to being mastered.

Students sometimes get caught up in using forms merely as a means to the next rank, but this is a mistake. By searching for the deeper understanding to be found in forms, your understanding of the spirit of Chung Do Kwan will also grow deeper.

In Pyong An 1 the opening move is a downward block, followed by a punch. You may have thought of this simply as a block followed by a strike, but before you have even executed the first downward block, you have already begun a self-defense response to being grabbed from behind (Figure 9-78). Chung Do Kwan forms begin with defensive moves first. This expresses the basic philosophy of not initiating attacks: "for defense only."

Figure 9-78

This form requires that both arms be raised and crossed at shoulder level to add power and protection to the downward block. But unwittingly, with a slight modification, this motion also begins to loosen the grip of an adversary who has grabbed you from behind (Figure 9-79). Your raised elbow combined with a push of the lower body gives you the space to pivot around and strike the opponent with a downward back-fist punch to the groin with your left hand, an adaptation of the downward block (Figure 9-80).

Figure 9-79

Figure 9-80

The next series in this form requires a turn of 180 degrees to perform the same two moves on the other side. This turn can be analyzed as a throw. As the attacker comes in with an attacking punch, you retreat one step as you block (Figure 9-81). You grab the punch, pivot on your right foot, and step behind toward the opposite side with your left foot so that you turn 180 degrees. The opponent is drawn forward, tripping over your right foot (Figure 9-82), and is then pulled down and thrown with the turn (Figure 9-83). This technique utilizes the principle of soft force, as in Aikido, where the force of the opponent's own punch is used to power his fall. You take down your opponent using skill in leverage. The mechanics of this throw are not taught until an advanced level, yet the basic training of reflexes for this advanced technique is begun at the white belt level. Full development of this skill will come later but is made easier by the early practice in the form. Every form contains hidden moves to be discovered over time. Students should engage in a personal searching process to distill insight from forms.

Figure 9-81

Strategies are also implied: the history of Tae Kwon Do shows that the Hwa Rang Do believed in never retreating in battle. This is evident in the beginning form, where blocks are performed while advancing.

Figure 9-82   Figure 9-83

These are just a few examples of alternate techniques and more general strategies hidden in the beginner form. Other techniques and strategies can be found at every level. We encourage you to make your own discoveries.

Analyzing Your Forms

You may wonder how to analyze your own forms to discover their hidden meanings. The more time you spend training in the martial arts, the easier such analysis becomes. Here are a few pathways to pursue. New students should ask their instructor for guidance.

Consider a block or punch not merely as the most obvious block or punch. Be willing to think about every move, including its direction and category, for meaning and possible variations. We have shown how a downward block can also be a strike. The chamber position is also an elbow strike to an opponent behind you. Allow your own ideas and those of your instructor to emerge. The values of your system may help you to unravel the hidden mysteries.

Look at what occurs between moves. Sometimes what seems to be background or nothing might become an important aspect to understand. Traditionally, insights were hidden from casual observers. Our point of view can influence what we see. Think about the history and background of your own system.

Shift your perspective when interpreting your forms. In Eastern philosophy, the concept of emptiness implies that the spaces between things are just as important as the things themselves. The motion used to prepare for a block or punch has applications in grappling, striking, blocking, and throwing. A pivot or a turn might also be a way to exert leverage to throw the opponent. The preparatory motion used to perform a block, such as knife-edge or double-arm block, may have significance of its own in grappling, soft blocks, and takedowns.

Learn by Doing

Leave some room for ambiguity in forms interpretation. Some learning takes place simply through doing. To overly classify and analyze a piece of art can sometimes detract from the enjoyment of it as a creation. Similarly, forms express the artistry of a style.

The experience of performing the movements will emerge indirectly in sparring. You will find that you have a multitude of responses, gained from the forms, which you can perform when needed. Sometimes you will plan a strategy or practice combinations, but at other times you know what to do automatically, without thought. While sparring, a creative answer to a situation can suddenly occur to you without conscious effort. The block or counterattack just seems to happen at exactly the right moment, in just the right way, but if you reflect upon it later, you will often recognize that the new move derived from your forms.

Practicing forms regularly with an open mind brings you into contact with many indirect teachings with practical results! The source is deep within, where intense meditative search has released your potential through forms.

Some may believe that they can accelerate their learning by attempting to learn vast numbers of form patterns. Maskelyne and Devant were two of the great magicians of the past whose skill in magic was impeccable. An ambitious novice who had spent countless waking hours studying innumerable quantities of illusions asked how many magic tricks these great master magicians knew. They replied simply, "About six!" The novice was shocked, to say the least. It is a mistake to assume that memorizing hundreds of movements are all that is required for mastery. Without knowledge of the basics and a corresponding depth of understanding that evolves from within, much is lost. Study your forms well and practice them over time. You may be surprised by the great benefits you receive from your efforts.

~ 10 ~

Three-Step Prearranged Sparring

> Where the mind goes, the body goes; so as soon as a
> face-off begins, you should shift your body to the
> appropriate spot like an image reflecting in a mirror.
>
> *Musashi*

Chung Do Kwan has developed special teaching methods for communicating the art to students. We learn just as our ancestors did many years ago; we practice as they did. And, thus, we transcend time and space, to partake in the original spirit of the style. By performing these methods, certain skills can be readily learned and passed down through present-day students to future generations. Practice will make perfect: anyone who puts forth the effort can master these skills, now or in the future.

One of these time-honored teaching methods is the three-step, a cornerstone of training. The three-step is a preplanned, two-person exercise in which partners take turns: one attacks and the other defends, followed by a finishing counterattack. The pace, distance, and use of technique are all safe and controlled, so both partners can experiment and learn in the process. This traditional teaching technique helps translate the solitary activities of practicing basics and forms into the realm of interaction with an opponent.

The three-step provides an opportunity to practice ideas for offense and defense. You may think of ways you could block or attack in sparring or self-defense, but you don't really know how effective these techniques will be until you try them. Because the three-step is preplanned and deliberate, many types of moves can be safely tried out. When you develop some effective ones, you can repeat them over and over until you train your reflexes to react spontaneously and accurately.

Another important benefit of the three-step is that it offers participants many opportunities to observe and follow both attacks and defenses. Untrained people will instinctively turn away from an incoming force directed right toward them.

The ability to face the force is fundamental for successful execution of powerful, focused techniques. During the three-step, the receiver learns how to watch the attack without flinching or looking away.

Ultimately, the three-step is a bridge between form and function, leading students from formal training to free sparring and self-defense. The three-step offers us a pathway to perfect our art, and thereby, a way to perfect ourselves.

Three-Step Fundamentals

The most basic three-step pattern involves defense against three upper-target punches. The attacker goes into a ready stance and signals readiness with a sharp yell. The defender yells in response when ready, and then the attacker advances with an upper-target punch (Figure 10-1). The defender pivots back to block from a defensive back stance. The attacker follows with a second punch, which the defender blocks, while stepping back (Figure 10-2). The attacker throws a third punch, which is also blocked from a back stance (Figure 10-3).

Figure 10-1

Now the defender is in position to counterattack. The attacker stands still to give the defender a chance to see openings, aim, and counterattack most effectively. In the first three-steps, a single counterattack is performed, such as one punch or one kick (Figure 10-4). Then the roles are reversed: the former attacker becomes defender, while the defender throws the punches.

Figure 10-2

Figure 10-3

Figure 10-4

Practice varied blocks and counters back and forth. Try all the blocks you have learned in basics and forms. All three-step patterns should be practiced on the left side and the right side. Attackers should vary by beginning with a left punch or a right punch so that you can try the pattern out on both sides.

Prearranged Three-Steps

Students are taught a few fundamental three-step patterns to give them some seed ideas. Once these are mastered, they may naturally start to think of variations. The second three-step involves the same defensive block, stepping backward 180 degrees in a back stance to defend against three punches. The counterattack is a knife-edge strike to several inches from the side of the neck of the opponent (Figure 10-5).

The third three-step begins with two blocks, as in the previous patterns. On the third punch, step back into a front stance and perform an X-rising block to deflect the punch upward (Figure 10-6). Throw a front kick toward the groin while continuing to hold the punch clamped in the X-block (Figure 10-7), and then press and guard the opponent's punching arm with the back of one hand, while performing a knife-edge strike toward the side of the neck (Figure 10-8).

Figure 10-5

Figure 10-6

Figure 10-7

Figure 10-8

Three-step patterns can also teach evasion. The first two blocks are performed as before, and then when the third punch comes in, a step back outside helps the practitioner to avoid the punch. A side kick can be directed toward the middle-target opening under the punching arm (Figure 10-9).

Figure 10-9

Creative Three-Steps

Different blocks move the opponent's punch in different ways. Notice how these variations combine with flowing counters. For example, a single-arm block from outside in (Figure 10-10) can create an opening for a counter to the opponent's middle- or upper-target area (Figure 10-11). For another variation, as the attacker comes in with a right upper-target punch, step back into a left back stance while blocking from outside in with a left single-arm block. After the third block pushes the opponent's arm in, an opening is created for a right reverse punch to the kidneys or a left roundhouse kick to the opponent's head. Try out all the different attacks you have learned, such as kicks, punches, knife-edge strike, and palm heel. Different blocks in various stances create corresponding openings for counterattacks.

Advanced Three-Steps

Advanced practitioners experiment with the advanced techniques they have learned in forms. But you can also apply advanced principles to the three-step.

Using the legs to block is one way to apply the crescent kicks from later forms. As the opponent comes in with a right-handed punch, bring your right foot around for an inward crescent kick, blocking the opponent's wrist (Figure 10-12). Step back and crescent kick all three attacks. The final counterattack can be a kick with the other foot or a secondary sidekick with the same foot to surprise the opponent (Figure 10-13). Front kicks can also be used for blocking. Kick up at the underside of the opponent's arm at the wrist to deflect the punch upward.

Figure 10-10

Figure 10-11

Figure 10-12

Figure 10-13

A simultaneous block-strike is another advanced concept that can be perfected in the three-step. For example, as the opponent comes in with a punch, block outward with a backhand block. Block the third punch, evading to the side in a front stance. Simultaneously, strike inside the punch with a sideways palm heel strike toward the chin or a knife-edge to the neck (see Figure 9-77). You utilize the opponent's incoming force against him, adding power to your own strike, while deflecting the incoming punch.

Takedowns can also be practiced in a three-step. Block the opponent's third right punch with an inward arm block in a right front stance (Figure 10-14), and then grab the opponent's wrist by hooking over it as you drop down on one knee and bring your left hand down to strike the back of the opponent's right leg (Figure 10-15) and sweep upward (Figure 10-16) as you take him down.

Figure 10-14

Figure 10-15

Figure 10-16

Double and triple counterattacks also add complexity to three-steps. The first counterattack sets up the second, followed by the third. This practice is very important for sparring, where it can be difficult to score on the first attack. Usually a series will be far more effective than a single attack.

One-Steps

One-steps are an advanced application that allows another variation. Practitioners can get a good workout from a quick, strong exchange of one-steps.

Subtle evasion is often superior to moving straight back, especially against a larger or stronger attacker. When the attacker throws a single punch, evade by stepping sideways as you block. Then throw a counter into the opening created by your block or the opponent's line of attack. If you step outside, you create different openings than if you step inside. By controlling where you step, you can set up for your counterattack.

Another useful variation is to work with diagonal positions. Try blocking after stepping back on a diagonal, safely out of the line of attack (Figure 10-17). A diagonal step away (Figure 10-18 positions you for longer-range counters such as kicks and punches. A diagonal step inward (Figure 10-19) will put you in place for close-range techniques such as elbow strikes (Figure 10-20). This makes possible a broader range of counterattacks to the opening thus created.

Figure 10-17

Figure 10-18

A diagonal line placed on the floor can guide the defender in his evasive stepping.

Figure 10-19

Figure 10-20

You can vary the position of attacker and defender. For example, both can be seated cross-legged, which restricts movements to blocks. Another variation is to do one-step from one knee. This position permits you to change orientation to block and counterattack.

Accuracy

Three-step practice perfects the dynamics needed for effective execution of the art in sparring and self-defense: accuracy, distance, and timing.

Accurate placement of blocks and counterattacks is essential if they are to really be effective. Attention to placement is the first step. When performing the three-step, it is important to look directly at the punch as it comes in, to confront attacks or counterattacks steadfastly, with discipline and courage.

Direct your attention to the punch, and place your block exactly where you want it. You can block more accurately if you watch the force coming toward you. When performing the beginning three-step exercise, block with the back of your hand. Deflect the opponent's punch exactly from the wrist zone. Bend your arm at the elbow at a right angle, elbow down and parallel to your side. Tense your arm and your lat muscles to maximize the use of body dynamics. If your arm is bent at the elbow less or more than 90 degrees, the block will be weaker. Advanced three-steps may use variations in the blocking point as well as its target, but the attacker's wrist area is the fundamental target for blocking.

Distance

The three-step teaches you how to apply your blocks and counterattacks at the correct distance. You must learn exactly how far your own arms and legs reach so that you can block with the best placement for your body dimensions. As you work with different-sized opponents, you will have to adjust your distance. Review the distance awareness exercise in chapter 3 to attune yourself to the length of your own arms and legs as a preliminary to sensing your distance for blocks and attacks.

Using the self-awareness gained from meditation, perform the three-step again. Notice how far you need to step away from the punch to evade it without having to overly extend your arms to block or counterattack. You should be in a balanced stance, with your arms positioned correctly for the block and counter you choose to use. This should become habit.

Where you step is just as important as how you step. Pay attention to how far you need to step in order to effectively evade the punch.

Timing

The precise timing of blocks and attacks can make the difference between effective and ineffective technique. You can improve your timing by practicing the three-step with varied partners. Everyone throws punches a little differently. You may have to speed up or slow down to meet each punch at the correct moment. And your distance from your opponent must be altered in order to block successfully.

You can improve your timing without a partner by using the timing exercise in chapter 3. Review this exercise, and then try your three-steps again. You may find that your three-step response is quicker.

Eventually, distance, timing, and accuracy become instinctive. Without thought, you will find yourself stepping, blocking, and countering your training partner. Three-step learning automatically translates into better sparring and more effective performance of self-defense techniques.

– 11 –

Free Sparring

In the moment of truth
As you begin to spar
You may discover
Just how you are.

C. Alexander Simpkins

Free sparring provides the opportunity for students to apply everything they have learned. Free sparring is the sport aspect of the art, permitting the creative, personal expression of techniques and their application to offense and defense in a safe, controlled setting. It is called free sparring because it gives students a chance to be freely creative. Fighting strategy comes from within. Mind and body react and act as one. When you carefully observe sparring, you will notice that each person is different. Their personalities are expressed in sparring as in any art. For example, one student may be quick to rush in, aggressively chasing the opponent. Another may be cautious, preferring to wait out the situation and counterattack at strategic moments. Each has an appropriate strategy and rhythm.

Free sparring should be done in a class under supervision of the instructor for safety and correct training. Students begin sparring as yellow belts to allow them time to develop the control and precision necessary for no-contact sparring. White belts watch with amazement and anticipation of their own eventual participation. As the black belts spar, observers see a continuous flow of power unleashed back and forth. Then, when the allotted one-minute time is over, the instructor claps two times, and the match ends in perfect precision with a polite controlled bow. Camaraderie and good will abound, as everyone shares in the training together.

No-Contact

In traditional martial arts, respect for origins is fundamental. There is an inner logic that technique is based in, although it is hidden from the perspective of those outside. Modern sport Tae Kwon Do uses various levels of contact, and subsequent stances, forms, and technique have been altered to support it. Many modern practitioners of Tae Kwon Do may not know that sparring practice of the original kwans in Korea was no-contact. Many Chung Do Kwan schools follow this tradition today. No-contact is the purest form of the art. It keeps the art from actually hurting anyone without sacrificing the ability to defend effectively. Here is the logic of this Way.

When Chung Do Kwan was formulated in Korea to unite and inspire its people, it was created as an "empty-hands 'Way.'" What this meant was that no offensive weapons could be used: no guns, no knives, no brass knuckles. No defensive armor was allowed either: no pads, no headgear, no arm or shin pads— nothing. Practitioners were forced to rely solely on their inner resources and skills, training with bare feet and bare hands throughout the workout.

Today, as in the past, students are taught to throw full-force kicks and punches without holding back, but to aim just about an inch from the uniform. If someone gets hit, then the practitioner is not performing the kick or punch properly: complete control and accuracy are expected and used as one of the fundamental criteria of excellence.

No-contact can be easily adapted to tournament scoring. Since no contact is made, full-power extension of techniques can be assessed. The quality of the attack can be judged and its power evaluated.

The force that Chung Do Kwan develops could be damaging, even lethal to the opponent if followed through, so for safety, a slight gap is better. In this way, sparring partners won't get hurt, while their power and focus can be developed and expressed. Performing techniques safely while using full force every day in practice will be an advantage. In this way, practitioners won't have to pull punches and kicks in order to avoid injuring each other—instead they control distance. Practitioners can trust their training partners, compete hard, and have great fun doing it.

Defense

Just as no-contact practitioners do not hit their opponent, they also do not allow their opponent to hit them. This enhances awareness of positioning and distance. Good, strong defense is an essential aspect of no-contact sparring.

For those who like the feeling of contact, there are always the blocks. In no-contact fighting, the block must connect. To truly stop a powerful punch or kick, the defender must use focus, stance, and positioning in every deflection. Practitioners must learn to perform a block just as effectively as a strike or it will not work. Some toughening of the arms and legs can help make it possible to stop a strong kick or punch with the blocking arm or take a strong block on the kicking leg without bruising. And no-contact training teaches control.

Training

How do students train to develop the varied skills needed for no-contact sparring? From the first *Choon-bi* to start the workout, to the final *Command Cho* and ending bow, sweat pours down in an intense workout. Everyone is roused to put forth full effort with every punch, block, and kick. Each technique should be performed fully. In order to develop the power required for this style, practitioners must not slack off. Through repetition at full intensity, everyone improves.

The workout also trains sparring skills. Each component is a building block to peak sparring performance. The basics, forms, and three-step included in every workout lead to developing skills for sparring.

Free-Sparring Guidelines

Good form is important when sparring. Chung Do Kwan is an art, not just an exchange of attacks and counterattacks. Sloppy or inaccurate technique is not a full expression of the art. Furthermore, a sloppy block will not work, and an inaccurate attack will fail to pass through the opponent's defense.

Stance has a profound effect on sparring technique. A large, powerful, or less-mobile practitioner will use stances differently from a small, quick, light practitioner. But both draw upon the same repertoire of stances, applied in their individual ways.

Stance leads to strategy. For example, a deep strong stance permits focused, strong blocks or attacks but may not be the best choice for quick fluid evasion. A shorter, lighter stance will be useful for moving in or out quickly. So most people use a combination of stances to respond to varied situations.

Defense is just as important as offense. A strong, stable block allows the defender to get an advantage. Retreat often leads to disadvantageous positioning.

Balanced, strong, and focused defense will allow for an effective, strategically placed counterattack.

If possible, stepping should be simple, used as a base. Always have this to fall back on and have personal variations. Side steps, angle steps, cross-steps, and leaps have been practiced over and over in basics, forms, and the three-step. Even though there is no standardization in sparring footwork, the patterns contained in forms can be adapted to sparring.

Offensive techniques are drawn from the alphabet of kicks, punches, and strikes. Offensive patterns can be created and practiced until they flow naturally. The three-step offers an opportunity to try them out. Practice your combinations. Combinations that fit with the values of Chung Do Kwan are best for this. If patterns are adapted to other systems, then they should fit with the types of movement from that style.

Free sparring is an art. Art cannot be explicitly taught; it must be expressed and developed. Thus you may get suggestions for combinations from others, but ultimately sparring is creative, in response to the moment. Rigid, rote drills may inhibit your creative flow. But repetition that allows for some variation will be helpful. Techniques can be learned, but must be adapted to the individual practitioner.

Fitness helps give you endurance and the capacity to make the techniques work. Sparring can be very demanding. Although it is usually only one minute in length, the intensity calls forth great effort. If you do the workout wholeheartedly, you will build your fitness naturally. Some supplementary jogging and light weight lifting may also be helpful for developing the endurance needed.

Beginning

At beginning levels, technique is simple and basic. Students must learn how to block each incoming attack. In the ready position in sparring, the practitioner should have at least one hand up (Figure 11-1). Beginners have a tendency to drop their hands when they perform a kick, leaving their head and body open to a counterattack. Practice kicking with at least one hand up to guard, ready to block, and be ready to block immediately after kicking (Figure 11-2). Blocking techniques can be practiced in the three-step.

Figure 11-1

Figure 11-2

Attacks will also be simple. Draw from the techniques you have already learned: front kick, side kick, roundhouse kick for feet, and punch and knife-edge for hands. You can also use combinations from the basics. For example, a side kick followed by another side kick or front kick, followed by a side kick have already been practiced over and over, making them natural for sparring combinations.

Figure 11-3 *The defender uses a double-arm block practiced in basics to the opponent's punch.*

Figure 11-4 *Then, he checks the opponent's wrist preventing a counter as he throws a roundhouse kick.*

Some beginners may find free sparring intimidating. And it can be! But they must face it anyway. When practitioners observe the attack as it comes in, they can follow what is happening and apply what they know to defend successfully (Figure 11-3 and 11-4). There is always an element of risk. But free sparring is a safe, controlled situation, where practitioners should respect each other. By competently coping over time, practitioners also develop inner strength. The Okinawan "bible" of martial arts, the *Bubishi*, states, "Lacking confidence about self-protection is the mind's subliminal message to the body that more training is necessary to overcome fear" (McCarthy 1995, 69).

Intermediate Levels

Intermediate students have begun to develop proficiency in the basic techniques. With this firm base, they can think more deeply about what they are learning. They begin to analyze different angles of approach to the target for each kick or hand attack. For example, the punch and front kick come in straight, so if the attacker's blocks have dropped, the kick or punch may get in. The roundhouse kick and knife-edge strike make a circular path inward, allowing the attack to come in around a defense. All the different techniques in the style offer many possibilities for varied angles and timing for attack and defense.

Intermediate practitioners will benefit from the effort made in planning a few combinations. Often the first attack will not get in, but by the second or third the opponent may be moving back and unable to defend. A kick followed by a punch, or two kicks, one high and one low, will force the opponent into a more challenging blocking situation (Figures 11-5, 11-6, and 11-7). Keep combinations simple. Better to do a few, well-focused and accurate offensive moves than too many, unfocused, inaccurate ones.

By the middle level, some techniques come more naturally than others. Some people have a certain talent such as naturally high kicks, strong punches, or spinning kicks. The particular talent, may show up over time or may be present from the beginning, but talents are discovered in action. For example, a female student appeared to be small and fragile. She never thought of herself as a strong person. However, her front kick was naturally forceful. She practiced her front kick diligently, making it a very fast and strong technique. Eventually, she was able to use it successfully to score in sparring. Talents develop by practicing the techniques that seem to have potential.

Figure 11-5 *The first attack is an upward punch, bringing the opponent's block up.*

Figure 11-6 *Next a middle-target side kick makes the opponent block low.*

Figure 11-7 *The third attack, an upper-target knife-edge, scores.*

Intermediate students usually become aware of their weaknesses as well as their strengths. They need to devote extra time to improving weak techniques. For example, most students commonly have one side that is better than the other. They should try to develop both sides rather than just the best one.

As students progress, they learn how to spar strategically. They can predict how opponents are likely to respond. Similarly to a game of chess, the practitioner can bring about certain reactions in the opponent, setting up the counter. For example, one can use the diagonal stepping rehearsed in the three-step. The defender steps diagonally outside the attack to block an upper-target punch (Figure 11-8). Then, the side kicks he throws to middle target is difficult for the opponent to block (Figure 11-9). Free sparring is not simply reactive. Control of distance and timing disrupts the opponent's usual rhythms. This requires self-control and awareness, which evolves over time. The sense of distance developed in the three-step transfers here. Footwork from forms can also be used to move in or out as needed for control of distance.

Figure 11-8

Figure 11-9

Advanced Level: Black Belt

> See first with the mind, then with the eyes, and
> finally with the body and limbs.
>
> *D. T. Suzuki*

At black-belt level, martial arts practice is just as much mental as it is physical. After years of deliberate, thoughtful, and rigorous training, including thinking of combinations, black belts come to a point when performing the art itself is second nature, beyond thought. Black belts almost seem to be able to anticipate what opponents will do before they do it. Reactions are immediate, and flow is uninterrupted. Techniques are direct and swift, with no holding back, yet perfectly controlled. Black belts possess a personal sense of style in what they do, expressed most noticeably in sparring.

Advanced students do not spar in fear or anger. Their emotions do not interfere with their response to what the opponent does. Sparring becomes the part of the workout when steady strength of mind in action is expressed.

> Nothing definite is thought, planned, striven for, desired, or expected, which aims in no particular direction and yet knows itself capable alike of the possible and impossible . . . this state, which is at bottom purposeless and egoless, was called by the master truly spiritual.
>
> *Herrigel*

All the technical skill comes together. The years of training are there, and the advanced practitioner no longer needs to think about the mechanics of each technique. The ultimate technique is freedom from technique: no-technique. Zen calls this emptiness, where movement flows from a deeper source within. "Emptiness is one-mind-ness, one-mind-ness is no-mind-ness, and it is no mind-ness that achieves wonders" (Suzuki 1959, 165). Fast, strong, intense, controlled power in motion, the creative moment of sparring unfolds as mastery of the art is expressed. From oneness with the interaction, free sparring evolves.

~ 12 ~

Training Methods

Practice is enlightenment.

Zen Master Dogen

First and foremost, practice: To improve, you *do* it. Theory is secondary. And always have a specific workout to do. When you go to a Chung Do Kwan class, you know what to expect. But you can also work out on your own, following the workout format, and derive many of the same benefits.

Many positive rewards can be gained from the workout. It can be done anywhere, inside or outdoors, and at any time. This makes it easy to fit in the workout around work and family responsibilities. Another benefit is that the practice is safe and good for the body. In fact, people of all ages can participate, from young children through to senior citizens, with proper teaching. You can practice alone, or share it with others.

All of these qualities make this art an enjoyable recreation with fringe benefits. If you do the workout regularly and try your best, you undergo a transformation, becoming more fit, flexible, coordinated, and strong. Your mind changes, too, as you gain focus, awareness, and quicker responses. All of these positive benefits generalize into healthier, calmer, and more confident everyday living. Discipline gained from practicing regularly helps you realize achievements of all kinds.

The Workout

Chung Do Kwan schools around the world will inevitably have their own variations of the workout. But commonly, they share in structured training, including some type of basics, forms, three-step, and sparring, which continue the tradition. The workout regime included here is drawn from our teacher Grandmaster Son's workout.

Warm-Ups

Warming up before you begin and warming down when you finish are important components of the workout. These preliminary exercises are intended to warm up your entire body, from head to toe. Special care is given to the legs, since kicking is a vital part of the workout.

Practice begins with a five-minute jog. In class, the students follow the instructor around the dojang in a circular path. Midway through the jog, the instructor switches direction by running through the center in a yin-yang pattern and then continuing to circle in the opposite direction. You can do this yourself, running first in one direction and then turning in a yin yang pattern to run in the other direction. Running both ways balances the body, working out the right and left sides equally.

Following the jog come stretches. Legs are stretched very carefully to prepare for their extensive use in kicks and stances. Leg stretches are performed by standing with legs a double shoulders' width apart, feet flat and facing forward. Place your hands on your knees. Bend one knee as you straighten the other, and push slightly over the straight leg to stretch the inside of the leg. Then, shift your weight to stretch the other leg. Next, pivot the foot of your straight leg so your heel rests on the floor and your foot points up. Gently push to stretch the back of your leg. Repeat on the other side. Now, turn ninety degrees and put the ball of your foot down on the straight leg for a gentle stretch to the front of your upper leg. Let your heel drop down to the floor, and you will stretch your calf. Repeat on the other side.

The remaining warm-ups are typical stretches used in many sports, covering the whole body.

Breathing Warm-Ups

Breathing is an integral part of the workout, so warming up the lungs is important. As you raise your arms out from your side, take in a full breath, moving the air all the way down to your abdomen. Exhale slowly as you bring your arms back down to your sides. Repeat three times.

Basics

Next comes a series of basic strikes and blocks, performed up and down the floor. Basics are the punches, kicks, and blocks that are the alphabet of movement. From this fundamental alphabet, the student will be able to combine these elements so they flow together in useful combinations to fluently express the spirit of Chung Do Kwan. This practice not only teaches the main punches, blocks, kicks, and combinations, but also gives practitioners a good cardiovascular and strength-building workout.

Students are taught all the basics at the beginning. Learning the general patterns is fairly quick, but perfecting them can take a lifetime. Even the highest-ranking black belt can always perform kicks and punches a little faster and a little stronger.

In class, everyone does basics together. Being a part of the thunderous group moving up and down the floor to count inspires everyone to try their best with each technique. But you can also practice the basics yourself at home or outdoors to get a good overall workout. See the chapters in part 2 for exact instructions on each technique.

Each basic is performed a fixed number of times, moving forward in stance with each technique, then turning about face, followed by one fewer repetition of the technique back, followed by turning about face to come back to the starting position. Breathe out with each extension, finishing during or at the point of muscle tension and focus. Breathe in with each retraction, relaxation, or preparation, between extensions. Remember to breathe in and out, with a natural rhythm, even though you are concentrating intensely on the action.

Begin in the ready position. Step forward with your left foot into a left front stance as you perform a left downward block. Then step forward into a right front stance as you throw a right punch. The target is a spot in the air at full extension from your arm, centered, at solar plexus level. Keep stepping forward for a total of seven punches. Then turn about face and perform six punches back, turn about face as you perform a downward block, then return to ready position. Pause and relax for a short time, about thirty seconds. Next comes the upper-target punch, performed exactly like the middle-target punch, except that the punch is aimed higher, at chin level.

Next comes a series of blocks that covers the middle and upper areas. An upward block is first. Step into a left front stance as you perform a left upward block. Step forward and perform seven consecutive upward blocks, then turn about face, do six back, turn about face, and come back to command. Perform a double-arm block the same way. The single-arm block is the exception. It begins with the right foot and right hand, to keep practitioners from becoming overly routine in their reactions.

Front kicks and side kicks are next. The front kick is preceded by a front stretch to limber the legs. Step into a left front stance (Figure 12-1), and then lift your back leg up in front, keeping your hips square ahead (Figure 12-2). Perform this seven times up and six back, as in the hand techniques. Follow this with front kicks. The side kick is performed in a horse stance, facing sideways. Cross-step and stretch the back leg sideways, keeping your foot parallel to the floor. Do six up and six back. Follow this with side kicks, performed from the horse stance.

A knife-edge block follows, in a back stance, and then a knife-edge strike also in back stance. Roundhouse kicks are then performed, in a front stance, bringing the foot down directly into the next front stance.

Finally, there are some combinations. Front kick, side kick is first. Begin with a left front kick, place your foot down, toe out. This turns your body, readying it for the side kick. Usually, where your foot points, your body follows. Then, execute a side kick with your right leg. Repeat the pattern down the floor, and then turn about face to return to your starting position.

A reverse punch combination is next. This basic begins with a left knife-edge strike in left back stance, followed immediately with a right punch. Perform both techniques in the stance without moving your feet. Notice how your punch comes off the back leg (called a reverse punch) for close-in encounters. Next, step into a right back stance and perform a right knife-edge block (Figure 12-3), followed immediately by a left reverse punch (Figure 12-4). Continue this basic with the knife-edge block, reverse punch combination.

Figure 12-1

Figure 12-2

Figure 12-3

Figure 12-4

The final combination, a six-step, is six consecutive moves, combining blocking, kicking, and punching. Start by stepping back with your right foot, and do a left knife-edge block (Figure 12-5). Step forward with your right foot into a right front stance, and perform a right punch (Figure 12-6). Then turn and throw a left turning side kick (Figure 12-7), followed by a right roundhouse kick (Figure 12-8) and then a left roundhouse kick (Figure 12-9). For the last move, step in for a right punch in a right front stance (Figure 12-10), with a resounding "yutz!"

Figure 12-5

Figure 12-6

Figure 12-7

Figure 12-8

Figure 12-9

Figure 12-10

Forms

Forms are the next part of the workout. You should perform the forms for your level and below only. You will not benefit from trying higher-level forms. Chung Do Kwan forms build, one upon the other, and skipping forms is like trying to build a house without a foundation.

Practice your forms first with count and then without count. The count goes from one to ten, and then begins again. Give one count to each technique in the early forms. Some of the advanced forms combine a few moves into one count, since practitioners are performing moves faster as they progress through the ranks. (See chapter 9 for the forms' instructions.)

Three-Step Sparring

Three-step sparring is the next part of the workout. You will need a partner to perform these exercises. When done in class, students line up in two lines facing each other, so each has a partner. Each pair works together for several minutes, until they hear a loud clap signaling that everyone should rotate to get a new partner. This gives students experience working with different opponents. In this way, they learn to adjust their technique so that they can deal with any size person and many varieties of attack. (See chapter 10 for details on the three-step.)

Free Sparring

Free Sparring is a continuous exchange of kicks and punches for one minute. Sometimes two-minute sparring is done to build extra endurance. This part of the workout is best done under the supervision of an instructor.

Once again, students line up facing each other. Sparring begins with a "bow, begin" called out by the instructor. After the match, students return to their double lines, bow, and then rotate to get a new partner. Occasionally, the instructor will have one pair spar as the class watches. You can learn from watching others just as you learn from actually sparring. (See chapter 11 for sparring instructions.)

Warm-Downs

The workout ends with warm-downs. Most people recognize the importance of warming up, but few realize how beneficial some simple stretches at the end of the workout can be. You will find that if you stretch after each workout, you will feel less sore and become more supple over time.

Warm-downs are similar to warm-ups, with one addition. The last exercise is a massage. Squat down over your heels, resting on the balls of your feet. Using your knife-edge, lightly tap your lower body. This part of the workout dates back to the original role of martial artists as both protectors and healers. After a few minutes of massage, everyone stands up and jumps up lightly into the air several times. The workout ends with a straightening of the lines and bowing to the instructor.

Supplementary Training

Many training methods supplement training so that practitioners learn how to take and give force without getting hurt or hurting others.

A seventy-pound heavy bag usually hangs in a Chung Do Kwan school, wrapped with duct tape to keep it going after the many powerful kicks and punches it has endured. You can hang your own heavy bag outdoors from a firm tree branch. Heavy bag training will help you build the strength of your techniques through hitting something solid. You can increase resistance by swinging the bag away from you and kicking or punching as it comes toward you. Keep your wrist and fist tight for punches and your foot and ankle tight for kicks.

Traditionally, a kwon go hangs on the wall or is wrapped around a post sunk into the ground. In the old days, a padded board was wrapped tightly with rope, but today you can purchase a kwon go from a martial arts supply store. Practice punches, kicks, and other hand strikes (Figures 12-11, 12-12, and 12-13). This will toughen your skin and bones. Strike five to ten times several times a week to gradually build your body. Be conservative in your training so that you do not overtrain, since injuries will only hold you back. Increase intensity gradually as you become more conditioned. Kicks can also be performed.

Figure 12-11

Figure 12-12

Figure 12-13

Modern innovations include other training aids such as a speed bag, body-shield pads, and other devices for improving the qualities of technique. Use whatever aids are available, but always perform your strikes your best.

Testing Training by Board Breaking

First-degree black belt tests require Chung Do Kwan students to break at least four boards. Women must break a minimum of three. High-ranking black belts break more. These consistent demonstrations of power among Chung Do Kwan practitioners show how this style does indeed build tremendous power.

The ability to break wood is a by-product of training. Practitioners can break wood because of regular, repeated workouts, not only from practice in board breaking itself. Properly guided and consistent conditioning is essential.

Board breaking should always be learned under careful supervision to guide you in the correct technique for doing it safely and successfully. For personal safety, do not attempt to break boards without an experienced teacher to instruct you in the process.

Kwon go training should be done to prepare for board breaking. Students train for several months before they attempt their first break. This extra training prepares the body for the impact and gives a better chance for success.

If you have properly trained in the basics, forms, three-step, and sparring, plus conditioned yourself correctly, breaking will go smoothly. A well-aimed, well-executed, and focused blow will break a board. Prepare carefully and well, and clear your mind of distractions. Then, you will not only be able to break wood but will also experience a Zen moment—fully focused in the present, mind and body becoming One (Figure 12-14).

Figure 12-14

— 13 —

Effective Self-Defense

> With wisdom and good sense, he guards his life
> from harm.
>
> *Ancient Chinese Book*
> *of Songs*

Self-defense in Chung Do Kwan is not fancy, exotic, or showy. But it gets the job done. Consistent with Chung Do Kwan's principles, self-defense methods are simple, direct, and powerful. Likewise, strategy should be simple to perform so that you can perform it well under any circumstances.

Whatever the practitioner does to respond to a self-defense situation should be powerful and decisive. Always trying hard, with every punch, kick, and block during practice makes a strong approach to self-defense a habit. Grandmaster Son states it more succinctly: "One kick or punch, finished."

Specific training for self-defense is essential. Strategies must guide the actions taken. But training should be in accord with the principles and criteria of Chung Do Kwan, not just a series of tricks and strategies. Do not seek a completely different kind of response from the many blocks, kicks, and hand attacks that you already practice. Each defensive move, as one would expect, should have speed, power, focus, balance, and accuracy and yet be relaxed at the correct time. Strike to the center and block to the center. Use these criteria in self-defense as you would in all techniques. Self-defense is not different; it is the same, just an extension of what you practice in the workout. Be consistent. For example, punch the arm that is in position to grab you, and kick the leg that tries to throw you.

Drills of moves for specific applications help to some extent, but every self-defense situation is a little different and requires a flexible response. Just practicing a specific technique may not adequately prepare the practitioner for real-life threats. Sometimes it is important to be able to problem solve in a fraction of a second, and adapt the technique you know to an unusual circumstance.

Traditionally no contact is the rule in free sparring. People often wonder how no-contact can be effective for self-defense. But the transition is natural and simple: No-contact practitioners simply adjust their distance by moving in closer to deal with the situation appropriately. Because they consistently perform every technique with full force in practice, their reflexes are ready when a powerful technique is needed. But so is their self-control. This leads to the correct attitude for self-defense.

Chung Do Kwan is a gentleman's art. To be a troublemaker is considered wrong: Morality is important. So self-defense means just that, *self*-defense. Do not initiate fights. Practitioners should not fight unless they are truly being threatened. And if they have been threatened, they should defend with composure and control, using their power correctly.

Practice self-defense under supervision. Learn correct habits, and get feedback so that your reactions are correct. Check with your instructor before you practice how to apply your techniques, to check the correctness of what you do, and to verify that the technique is appropriate.

Use restraint and self-discipline. An old saying from Chinese martial arts applies here: "No first punch, no second punch." The practitioner does not initiate conflict or "throw the first punch." But the attacker should not be given an opportunity to throw another, second, punch. Blocks and counterattacks should prevent this. But be aware of the consequences of your actions. Federal and local laws apply to self-defense. For example, the law prohibits people from maiming or harming others. This works both ways. Self-defense is rarely an all-or-nothing situation. Extreme actions are usually only necessary in extreme situations. The response must not be out of proportion. Choose wisely. But once the decision is made, do not hesitate. Just react appropriately, without pause.

Areas of Vulnerability

All people have points of vulnerability, also known as pressure points. Your instructor can direct you, but a few examples, shown in the techniques, will help to point the way. An accurately placed strike to a pressure point can stop an attacker from continuing, or cause the attacker to release the defender from a hold.

Beginners are initially taught simple, direct, powerful counters to general areas. After all, a white belt cannot expect to aim well and control exact placement of punches and kicks. An attempt to strike or block to an upper, middle, or lower target begins the development of control. Later, when advanced practitioners have gained control over the exact placement of their techniques, they choose more precise targets.

Types of Self-Defense Situations

For the purpose of simplification, self-defense situations may be considered a defense against empty-handed attacks or attacks against weapons. Empty-handed attacks include punches, kicks, holds, grabs, throws, and takedowns. Weapon attacks may be further divided into cutting/slashing with knives or spears, strikes with clubs or sticks, and threats with guns. Because of the scope of this book, we will not deal with weapons here. For instruction on weapon defense, readers are encouraged to search for sources devoted to these situations, such as Son and Clark's books. Although you can apply Chung Do Kwan techniques to weapon defense, modifications are often needed to deal with these special situations.

Although there are general as well as specific rules you can follow, each situation encountered in self-defense is also unique. The attack may vary in many ways. And the defense has to take many variables into account. We will give examples of approaches, but because of these factors, it is always necessary to adapt and improvise with these methods to make them work.

Defense against Punches and Kicks

Chung Do Kwan trains practitioners well for defense against regular punches or kicks. You can use the blocks that you already know and have practiced often. But be aware that punches and kicks from a street attacker may not be thrown with strict form. A fight can have many surprises and may be unpredictable. Discipline is needed in order to develop the correct form that your training partners have.

Follow the safety rules you have already learned. Don't let the block move too far out away from your body or you could leave yourself open. To discourage the attacker from continuing, make each block count with good focus and power. A strong block hurts the opponent like a strike. Follow your block with a powerful punch or kick as a counterattack. Sometimes attacks must be stopped by a counter, not just blocked or evaded. Try to step outside of the attack to place yourself out of range from further attacks (Figure 13-1). The counter should be decisive and appropriate.

Whenever you kick, keep in mind that your attempts to counterattack offer an opening for a return counterattack. The counter may be at knee, hip, groin, midsection, or upper level. Be especially careful when kicking to a target above the waist because your balance is more precarious, potentially giving your opponent an opportunity to throw you. The conservative response is usually the safer one, unless you are unusually proficient with high kicks. This is often discouraged in situations that are potentially dangerous.

Figure 13-1 *The defender steps outside the attacker's punch and uses a strong outward block.*

Multiple Attackers

Defense against multiple attackers at brown belt level can be practiced with two-on-one sparring. Multiple attackers pose special issues, which an advanced book can address in more detail, but certain principles apply. Training in quick reactions, stepping and evasion, and strong technique can be very helpful for handling multiple attackers.

Keep moving. You must be more mobile when defending against two or more people so that you do not permit yourself to be surrounded. Ideally, try to line up the opponents so that you can handle them one at a time. If you do get surrounded, you must utilize your skills with simultaneous block/strikes that are developed from purple belt on. As you block one person, kick the other to push him away.

You must be especially alert to grab attempts so that you can avoid them. Break out of a hold as soon as an opponent attempts to apply it.

Defending against Grabs

The opponent may attempt to grab one wrist, both wrists, your arms, torso, neck, or other part of your body to exert dominance and produce pain or compliance with demands, or perhaps preparatory to a hold or lock. Chung Do Kwan offers a wide range of possible responses, so we will illustrate a few examples you can work out strategies from.

First, keep in mind that the forms, basics, and three-step suggest many possible pathways. In response to an attack, choose appropriately, and then vary your response to fit the circumstance. Hidden in the forms are many possible releases from holds. At each level of training, you must analyze and search for the correct release. Later, after years of drill and practice of the forms, you will have developed an understanding of the methods that work best for you. But we all begin with analyzing and problem solving, until such approaches become clear.

Any grab or hold has a weak point, a point of vulnerability for breaking out of it. The grasp on a wrist is weak at the thumb rather than the fingers—four digits versus one. Use the moves from a form to release from the hold. If your wrist is grabbed (Figure 13-2), perform a strong, focused, small circular motion to pull the holder's thumb open from the grip (Figure 13-3). To break out of a strong grip requires a sudden, focused reaction. You can practice releasing from a grab with a training partner. To prevent further attack, come down on the attacker's wrist and foot (Figure 13-4).

Figure 13-2

Figure 13-3   **Figure 13-4**

If your opponent tries to place you in a hold from the rear, step forward and drop your chin down to prevent the opponent from being able to choke you (Figure 13-5). Twist hard and fast to one side, and elbow the assailant. Twist to the other side and strike over your shoulder with an elbow to the opponent's upper-target area (Figure 13-6). Twist again to strike behind with another elbow to the middle target of the opponent. Keep alternating, with high and low elbow strikes until release is accomplished (Figure 13-7). The opponent should find it very uncomfortable to continue holding you as this barrage of counterattacks connects.

Pyong An 4 offers a strong counterattack to defend against a tackle from the front for a throw. This technique can also be used against an attempt to put you into a front bear hug. As the opponent advances to grab you, block outward with both arms (Figure 13-8). Then, reach out and grab the opponent's collar, with both hands if possible, and forcefully kick with a front kick to the opponent's midsection (Figure 13-9).

If the opponent bends forward and tries to tackle you, block the attempt by moving both arms upward and outward, then reach behind the opponent's upper body and draw it in or downward while lifting your knee upward toward the opponent's midsection. The pull in adds substantial extra impact to your counterattacking knee kick.

Another possible response is to turn and side kick toward the attacker as he extends his hands to grab (Figure 13-10). An opening is created between the opponent's outreaching arms. Be sure to plant your supporting leg firmly in place and do not lean away for height, as this can put you off balance, making you easier to throw.

Figure 13-5

Figure 13-6

Figure 13-7

Figure 13-8

Figure 13-9

Figure 13-10

The opening double blocks of Pyong An 4 can be modified to lock an opponent for self-defense. The defender grabs the attacker's punch as he blocks (Figure 13-11) and then twists to lock the attacker's elbow (Figure 13-12).

Figure 13-11

Figure 13-12

As your understanding of your martial art expands with repeated practice and sincere, thoughtful involvement, you will find yourself understanding the moves on a deeper level. You will not only develop the ability to respond correctly to situations but will also have trained your skills to make your techniques effective.

Conclusion

Chung Do Kwan spirit grows as many strong practitioners continue to carry on the traditions. If you want to get the most out of this art, practice hard. Always do your best. Don't waver, even if you feel tired or distracted by other things. Over time, your sincere efforts will be rewarded in many ways.

We hope that you will discover your own inner power and develop it for positive purposes. As Confucius said, "The man of moral virtue, wishing to stand firm himself, will lend firmness unto others" (Giles 1998, 60).